JUMP Math 4.2
Book 4 Part 2 of 2

D0517554

Contents

jump math™
MULTIPLYING POTENTIAL.

JUMP Math
One Yonge Street, Suite 1014
Toronto, Ontario M5E 1E5
Canada
www.jumpmath.org

Writers: Dr. Heather Betel, Julie Lorinc
Editors: Megan Burns, Liane Tsui, Natalie Francis, Lindsay Karpenko, Daniel Polowin,
          Susan Bindernagel, Holly Dickinson, Jackie Dulson, Dawn Hunter
Layout and Illustrations: Linh Lam, Fely Guinasao-Fernandes, Sawyer Paul, Klaudia Bednarczyk,
          Marijke Friesen, Gabriella Kerr, Huy Lam
Cover Design: Blakeley Words+Pictures
Cover Photograph: © Phongphan/Shutterstock

ISBN 978-1-928134-93-0

Second printing June 2019

Printed and bound in Canada

Welcome to JUMP Math

Entering the world of JUMP Math means believing that every child has the capacity to be fully numerate and to love math. Founder and mathematician John Mighton has used this premise to develop his innovative teaching method. The resulting resources isolate and describe concepts so clearly and incrementally that everyone can understand them.

JUMP Math is comprised of Teacher Resources, Digital Lesson Slides, student Assessment & Practice Books, assessment tools, outreach programs, and professional development. All of this is presented on the JUMP Math website: **www.jumpmath.org**.

The Teacher Resource is available on the website for free use. Read the introduction to the Teacher Resource before you begin using these materials. This will ensure that you understand both the philosophy and the methodology of JUMP Math. The Assessment & Practice Books are designed for use by students, with adult guidance. Each student will have unique needs and it is important to provide the student with the appropriate support and encouragement as he or she works through the material.

Allow students to discover the concepts by themselves as much as possible. Mathematical discoveries can be made in small, incremental steps. The discovery of a new step is like untangling the parts of a puzzle. It is exciting and rewarding.

Students will need to answer the questions marked with a ▯ in a notebook. Grid paper notebooks should always be on hand for answering extra questions or when additional room for calculation is needed.

Contents

Unit 5: Patterns and Algebra: Patterns

Unit 6: Number Sense: Multiplication

Unit 7: Number Sense: Division

PART 2

Unit 8: Probability and Data Management: Graphs

Unit 9: Number Sense: Fractions

Unit 10: Number Sense: Decimals

Unit 11: Patterns and Algebra: Equations

Unit 12: Measurement: 2-D Shapes

Unit 13: Measurement: Time

Unit 14: Geometry: 3-D Shapes

Unit 15: Probability and Data Management: Probability

PDM4-1 Gathering Data

> **REMINDER:** Data you collect yourself is called **primary** (or **first-hand**) data.
> Data collected by someone else is called **secondary** (or **second-hand**) data.

1. How would you collect the primary data? Write the letter for your choice.

   A. survey   **B.** observation   **C.** measurement

   a) How does the temperature of a cup of heated water change over time? __B__

   b) What are your classmates' favourite movies? __A__

   c) How far can the students in your class jump? __C__

   d) How many students in your class have brown hair? __A__

   e) Do you think it will rain in the next 20 minutes? __no__

2. Would you use primary or secondary data to answer the question?

   a) What is the average temperature where you live? __-3 °C_____

   b) How old are the students in your class? _____

   c) How many medals has Canada won in the last five Olympics? _____

   d) Which city gets more hours of sunlight, Calgary or Winnipeg? _____

   e) How do most students in your class get to school? _____

   f) How do most students in Canada get to school? _____

3. How is the data in Question 2 collected?

   A. survey   **B.** observation   **C.** measurement

   a) _____   b) _____   c) _____   d) _____   e) _____   f) _____

4. Are all possible responses given? If not, add an "other" category.

   a) What is your favourite sport?

      ☐ hockey ☐ volleyball ☐ basketball

   b) What is your favourite season?

      ☐ spring ☐ summer ☐ fall ☐ winter

   c) What is your favourite colour?

      ☐ blue ☐ red ☐ yellow

   d) What is your favourite primary colour?

      ☐ blue ☐ red ☐ yellow

5. Would everyone know the answer to the question? Write "yes" or "no" to answer.

   a) What's your favourite colour? _____   b) On what day of the week were you born? _____

   c) When is your birthday? _____   d) What's your eyeglass prescription? _____

6. Add a category so that everyone can answer the question.

   a) What is your favourite pizza topping?

   ☐ pepperoni ☐ pineapple ☐ mushroom ☐ _____

   b) In which season were you born?

   ☐ winter ☐ spring ☐ summer ☐ _____

   c) Which of these colours do you like best?

   ☐ red ☐ yellow ☐ blue ☐ green ☐ _____

   d) How tall are you?

   ☐ under 1.2 m ☐ 1.2 to 1.3 m ☐ 1.3 to 1.4 m ☐ 1.4 to 1.5 m ☐ _____

7. a) Write a survey question to ask students in your class.

   _____

   _____

   b) Write the possible responses to your question.

   ☐ _____   ☐ _____

   ☐ _____   ☐ _____

   ☐ _____   ☐ _____

8. a) Write a question that you will need secondary data to answer.

   _____

   _____

   _____

   b) Why can't you collect the data yourself?

   _____

   _____

   _____

PDM4-2 Pictographs

A **scale** shows what the symbol means on a pictograph.
10 students eat lunch at home and 20 students eat lunch at school.
Both pictographs show the same data, but they use different scales.

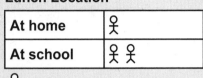

Lunch Location

| At home | ♀ |
| At school | ♀ ♀ |

♀ = 10 students ←——— scale ———→ ♀ = 5 students

Lunch Location

| At home | ♀ ♀ |
| At school | ♀ ♀ ♀ ♀ |

1. Look at the scale and multiply to find what the group of symbols means.

   a) ♀ = 5 people

   ♀ ♀ ♀ ♀ = _____ people   ♀ ♀ ♀ ♀ ♀ ♀ = _____ people

   b) ❈ = 7 flowers

   ❈ ❈ ❈ = _____ flowers   ❈ ❈ ❈ ❈ ❈ ❈ = _____ flowers

2. ☐ = 5 boxes. Draw symbols to show the number.

   a) 15 boxes =   b) 30 boxes =   c) 5 boxes =

3. a) Use the pictograph to fill in the table.

   Flowers in Evan's Garden   ❀ = 5 flowers

   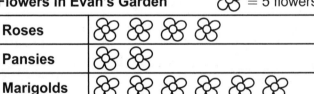

Roses	❀ ❀ ❀ ❀
Pansies	❀ ❀
Marigolds	❀ ❀ ❀ ❀ ❀ ❀

Type of Flower	Number of Flowers
Roses	
Pansies	
Marigolds	

   b) Use the data in part a) to draw a pictograph with the new scale.

   Flowers in Evan's Garden   ❀ = 10 flowers

Roses	
Pansies	
Marigolds	

   c) How many flowers does Evan have in total? _____

   d) Evan used the flowers to plant 5 identical flower beds. How many of each type of
      flower does he have in each bed?

   Roses: _____   Pansies: _____   Marigolds: _____

Half a symbol means half the number. Example: If ☺ = 4, then (= 4 ÷ 2 = 2.

4. The first row shows what ☺ means. What does (mean? Fill in the table.

☺	10	20	8	50	30	6	12
(							

5. The first row shows what one symbol means. What does each group of symbols mean?

a)

☆			2	10	100
☆ ✦					
☆ ☆ ☆ ✦					
☆ ☆ ☆ ☆ ✦					

b)

☖			8	20	12
☖ ☖)					
☖ ☖ ☖ ☖)					
☖ ☖ ☖ ☖ ☖ ☖)					

6. a) Use the pictograph to fill in the table.

How Students Get to School

Car	☖ ☖ ☖
Bus	☖ ☖ ☖ ☖ ☖ ☖ ☖)
Bike	☖ ☖)
Walk	☖ ☖ ☖ ☖ ☖

☖ = 10 students

Mode of Transportation	Number of Students
Car	
Bus	
Bike	
Walk	

b) How many students were surveyed? _____

c) How many times as many students walk as take a car? _____

d) How many more students take the bus than walk? _____

e) Fill in the Carroll diagram with the number of students whose transportation to school is in each category.

	Has an Engine	Does Not Have an Engine
Has Wheels		
Does Not Have Wheels		

BONUS ▶ Name a means of transportation that has an engine but no wheels.

_____

PDM4-3 Creating Pictographs

1. a) Count the tallies and draw a pictograph with the given scale.

   Plant

   Roses: 卌 卌 卌 卌 卌 卌 卌 卌   = _____ roses

   Pansies: 卌 卌 卌 卌 卌   = _____ pansies

   Dandelions: 卌 卌   = _____ dandelions

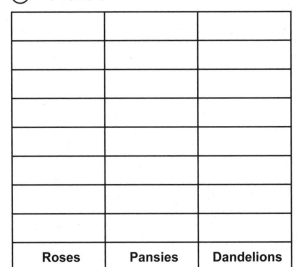

   i) ◯ = 5 flowers

Roses	**Pansies**	**Dandelions**

   ii) ◯ = 10 flowers

Roses	**Pansies**	**Dandelions**

   b) How many times as many roses as dandelions are there? _____

   c) Choose a title for the pictographs.

   _____

2. The first line shows the data. Circle the scale that works best for the data.

   a) 12, 4, 18, 6
   ♡ = 2
   ♡ = 3
   ♡ = 5
   ♡ = 10

   b) 30, 90, 60, 105
   ♡ = 2
   ♡ = 3
   ♡ = 5
   ♡ = 10

   c) 9, 12, 6, 27
   ♡ = 2
   ♡ = 3
   ♡ = 5
   ♡ = 10

   d) 25, 10, 35, 15
   ♡ = 2
   ♡ = 3
   ♡ = 5
   ♡ = 10

3. In Question 2.b), what would be your second choice for the scale? Explain.

   _____

   _____

   _____

4. A birdwatcher made a tally of the birds she saw on her trip.
Create a pictograph of the data.

a) Tally the data.

Bird

Robins: |||| |||| |||| |||| |||| |||| |||| |||| _____

Jays: |||| |||| |||| |||| |||| _____

Sparrows: |||| |||| |||| |||| |||| |||| |||| |||| |||| |||| _____

Finches: |||| |||| |||| _____

b) Fill in the title and labels on the pictograph.

c) Choose a symbol and a scale.

d) Complete the pictograph.

Title: _____

Scale: _____ = _____ birds

Bird

e) Order the birds from most to least common.

_____   _____   _____   _____

f) How many birds were seen in total? _____

g) Which two types of birds together make up half the birds seen? _____

h) Which type of bird was seen exactly twice as often as another type? _____

i) How many more sparrows than finches were seen? _____

j) How many more sparrows and robins were seen than jays and finches? _____

k) Make up your own question from the pictograph. Write the answer.

_____

_____

_____

PDM4-4 Bar Graphs

1. The bar graph shows approximately how many barrels of oil are used per person, each year, on every continent.

Oil Consumption per Person by Continent

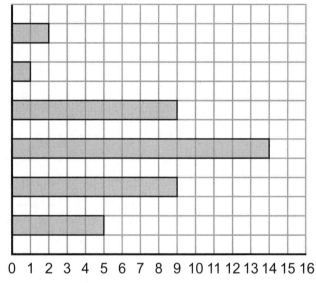

Barrels of Oil Used per Person in a Year

a) Which continent uses the least oil per person? _____

b) Which continent uses the most oil per person?_____

c) How many times as much oil does Asia use as Africa? _____

d) Which two continents use the same amount of oil? _____

e) How many barrels of oil per person per year does Europe use? _____

2. Rick asked his classmates if they liked travelling by car, plane, or train the most. He showed the answers in a bar graph.

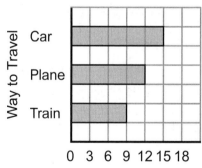

Number of Students

a) What number does the scale count by? _____

b) How many students prefer to travel by train? _____

c) How many more students prefer the car to the plane? _____

d) How many students were surveyed altogether? _____

BONUS ▶ Could a bar on this graph end in the middle of a block? Explain.

_____

_____

A bar can end between two numbers on a bar graph.

3. Students voted for their favourite summer activity. The bar graph shows the results.

   a) Fill in the table.

Favourite Activity	Number of Students
Baseball	5
Soccer	
Swimming	
Windsurfing	

Favourite Summer Activity

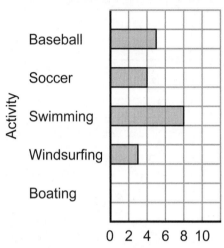

   b) 9 students picked boating. Add this to the table.
      Add the bar for boating to the bar graph.

   c) Fill in the blank.

      i) _____ times as many students picked boating as windsurfing.

      ii) _____ times as many students picked swimming as soccer.

      iii) _____ students picked water activities.

      iv) _____ times as many students chose water activities as soccer.

      v) _____ was the most popular activity.

      vi) _____ was the least popular activity.

      vii) How many students were surveyed? _____

   BONUS ▶

   d) Kyle thinks that the bar for swimming is 2 blocks longer than the bar for soccer,
      so 2 more students voted for swimming. Is he correct? Explain.

      _____

      _____

      _____

   e) On Sports Day, the class can choose three of these activities.
      Which three should they choose? Explain.

      _____

      _____

PDM4-5 Creating Bar Graphs

1. Sara is researching different dog breeds.

   a) Fill in the table using Bar Graph 1.

Dog Breed	Mass (kg)
Beagle (B)	
Collie (C)	
Dalmatian (D)	
Husky (H)	
Pug (P)	

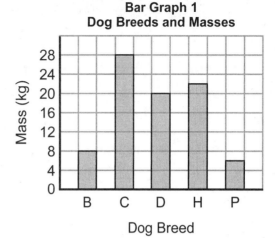

Bar Graph 1
Dog Breeds and Masses

   b) What number does the scale skip count by? _____

   c) Are there bars that end between the numbers? _____

   d) How many blocks long is the tallest bar? _____

   e) Use the table to complete Bar Graph 2 with
      a scale that skip counts by 2 to show
      the same information.

   f) Are there bars that end between

      the numbers? _____

   g) Which graph takes more space? _____

   h) Use the graphs to find out which dog
      breed has a mass 8 kg greater than
      a dalmatian.

      _____

      Which graph makes this easier

      to answer? _____

   i) Use the graphs to find out which
      breed weighs 22 kg less than a collie.

      _____

      Which graph makes this easier

      to answer? _____

   j) How much would 2 beagles, 1 collie, 1 dalmation,

      2 huskies, and 3 pugs weigh altogether? _____

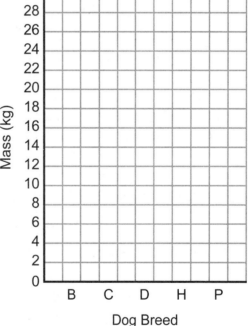

Bar Graph 2
Dog Breeds and Masses

2. Tasha surveyed her grade about their favourite pizza. She gave students four choices.

a) Here are the results of Tasha's survey. Tally the data.

Plain cheese: ~~||||~~ ~~||||~~ ~~||||~~ ~~||||~~ ~~||||~~ ~~||||~~   _____

Pepperoni: ~~||||~~ ~~||||~~ ~~||||~~ ~~||||~~ ~~||||~~ ~~||||~~ ~~||||~~   _____

Hawaiian: ~~||||~~ ~~||||~~ ~~||||~~   _____

Vegetarian: ~~||||~~ ~~||||~~ ~~||||~~ ~~||||~~ ~~||||~~ ~~||||~~ ~~||||~~ ~~||||~~ ~~||||~~   _____

b) Fill in the title and axis labels on the bar graph.

c) Choose a number to count by. Fill in the numbers on the axis.

d) Complete the bar graph.

Title: _____

_____

Plain Cheese										
Pepperoni										
Hawaiian										
Vegetarian										

0   __   __   __   __   __   __   __   __   __   __

_____

e) Write the pizzas in order from most to least popular.

_____   _____   _____   _____

f) How many students were surveyed altogether? _____

g) How many times as many people preferred vegetarian to Hawaiian? _____

h) How many times as many people preferred plain cheese to Hawaiian? _____

BONUS ▶ Tasha uses the information in Question 2 to buy pizzas for her grade.

a) If 1 pizza can feed 5 people, how many pizzas should she buy? _____

b) How many of each type of pizza should she buy?

Plain: _____   Pepperoni: _____   Hawaiian: _____   Vegetarian: _____

c) If 1 pizza can feed 8 people, how many of each type should she buy?

Plain: _____   Pepperoni: _____   Hawaiian: _____   Vegetarian: _____

PDM4-6 Double Bar Graphs

1. The double bar graph compares the average monthly snowfall in Ottawa and Winnipeg.

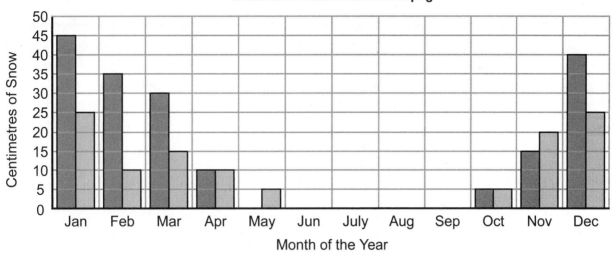

Snowfall in Ottawa and Winnipeg

a) In which months of the year does Winnipeg get more snow than Ottawa? _____

b) Which city gets more snow overall? _____

c) How much more snow does it get? _____

d) In which months does Ottawa get at least twice as much snow as Winnipeg?

_____

e) Which city has a longer winter? Explain.

_____

_____

_____

2. Would the comparison be suitable for a double bar graph? Explain.

a) Compare the heights to weights of students by age.

_____

_____

_____

b) Compare favourite movies of Grade 1 and Grade 6 students.

_____

_____

_____

3. Two Grade 4 classes challenged each other to collect food for a food bank for a week. Both classes kept track of how many cans were brought in each day.

	Monday	Tuesday	Wednesday	Thursday	Friday
Ms. Ali's class	6	12	18	34	60
Mr. Brown's class	30	22	26	20	32

a) Choose a colour to use for Ms. Ali's class, and colour in the box next to her name. Then use that colour to show the data in the double bar graph.

b) Choose a different colour for Mr. Brown's class. Add the data to the double bar graph.

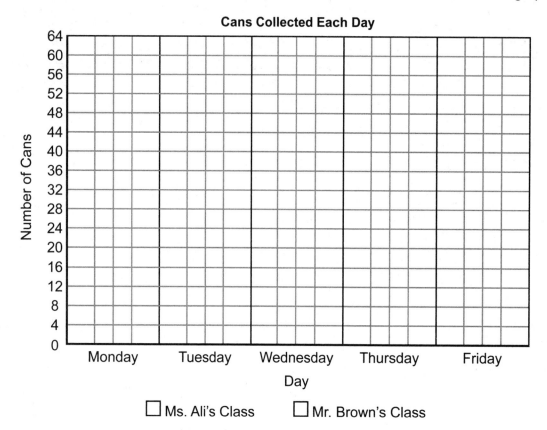

c) Which class collected the most cans of food? _____

d) In one class, a parent volunteered to help by collecting cans of food at home and bringing them by car at the end of the week.

In which class do you think this happened? _____

e) On which day did Mr. Brown's class bring 5 times as much food as Ms. Ali's? _____

f) On which day did Ms. Ali's class bring almost twice as much food as Mr. Brown's? _____

PDM4-7 Stem and Leaf Plots

The **leaf** of a number is its right-most digit.
The **stem** is all its digits except the right-most digit.
The stem of a one-digit number is 0 since there are no digits
except the right-most one.

stem   leaf

1. Underline the leaf.

    a) 1 2 <u>3</u>   b) 3 1   c) 7 2   d) 4   e) 3 8

    f) 9 0   g) 8 0 1   h) 4 4 4   i) 3 2 2 9 5   j) 4 3 4 1

2. Circle the stem.

    a) ⓪ 5   b) 3 7   c) 1 2 3   d) 3 1   e) 5 9 8 7 3

    f) 1 8   g) 6   h) 1 0   i) 4 3 2 1   j) 9 0 0 0

3. Underline the leaf and circle the stem.

    a) 8   b) 8 3   c) 8 3 1   d) 8 3 1 0   e) 4 0 7 1

    f) 6 8 9   g) 9 0 7   h) 8 9 9   i) 3   j) 6 2 4 5 9

4. Write a number with leaf 0: _____. Write a number with stem 0: _____.

5. Underline the numbers that have the same stem.

    a) 78, 74, 94   b) 89, 90, 91   c) 77, 67, 76

    d) 371, 379, 391   e) 263, 26, 265   f) 39, 390, 394

    g) 5782, 578, 574   h) 34, 341, 3, 340   i) 291, 287, 28, 29

6. Circle the stems. Then write the stems from smallest to largest.

    a) 13 9 8 24 64 18 25   b) 26 29 48 53 27 9 44   c) 99 134 136 128 104 97

    ____, ____, ____, ____   ____, ____, ____, ____   ____, ____, ____, ____

BONUS ▶ a) Do numbers with the same stem have the same number of digits? Explain.

_____

_____

   b) Do numbers with the same leaf have the same number of digits? Explain.

_____

_____

To build a stem and leaf plot for the data set 38, 29, 26, 42, 43, 34:

Step 1: Find the stems. The stems are 2, 3, and 4.

Step 2: Write the stems from smallest to largest.

Stem	Leaf
2	
3	
4	

Step 3: Write the leaves for each stem in the leaf column.

Stem	Leaf
2	9 6
3	8 4
4	2 3

Step 4: Order the leaves by row from smallest to largest.

Stem	Leaf
2	6 9
3	4 8
4	2 3

7. Put the leaves in the correct order. Then list the data from smallest to largest.

a)

Stem	Leaf
2	4 1
3	8 6 5
4	3 2

→

Stem	Leaf
2	1 4

____, ____, ____, ____, ____, ____, ____

b)

Stem	Leaf
0	4
1	9 5
2	3 8 0

→

Stem	Leaf

____, ____, ____, ____, ____, ____

c)

Stem	Leaf
8	3 0
9	0 7 2
10	6

→

Stem	Leaf

____, ____, ____, ____, ____, ____

d)

Stem	Leaf
9	2 1 8
10	4 2 4
11	5 0

→

Stem	Leaf

____, ____, ____, ____, ____, ____, ____, ____

8. Create a stem and leaf plot from the data.

a) 9, 7, 12, 19, 10

Stem	Leaf

→

Stem	Leaf

b) 99, 98, 102, 99, 101

Stem	Leaf

→

Stem	Leaf

9. Anna and some friends ran a 5 km race. Their recorded times were 26, 32, 38, 29, and 40.

a) What unit of measurement do you think they used: seconds, minutes, hours, or days? _____

b) Make a stem and leaf plot of the data.

Probability and Data Management 4-7

PDM4-8 Range, Median, and Mode

> The **range** of a data set is the difference between the largest and the smallest data values.
> Example: The range of 3, 7, 9, 4 is $9 - 3 = 6$.

1. Find the range of the data set.

   a) 6, 9, 4, 12, 5   b) 7, 4, 8, 6, 11, 9   c) 42, 39, 36, 41, 41

   _____ − _____ = _____   _____ − _____ = _____   _____ − _____ = _____

> The **median** of a data set is the middle number when the data is arranged in order.
> To find the median, put the data in order. Cross out from either end until you reach the middle.
> Example:
>
> $$\not{2} \quad \not{3} \quad ⑥ \quad \not{7} \quad \not{11}$$
> The median is 6.

2. Circle the median of the data set.

   a) 1, 5, 12, 31, 42   b) 3, 4, 6, 8, 11, 13, 13   c) 2, 2, 8   d) 21, 123, 144, 167, 932

> If there are two middle numbers, the median is halfway between the two numbers.
> Example:
>
> $$4 \quad 6 \quad ⟨7 \quad 9⟩ \quad 10 \quad 11$$
> The median is 8 because $9 - 8 = 8 - 7$, so 8 is halfway between 7 and 9.

3. Find the number that is halfway between the given numbers.

   a) 6 and 8   b) 13 and 15   c) 40 and 44   d) 10 and 20   e) 35 and 45   f) 63 and 73

   _____   _____   _____   _____   _____   _____

4. Circle the middle number or numbers. Find the median.

   a) 2, 4, 6, 7, 8   b) 2, 3, 3, 8

   _____   _____

   c) 7, 9, 13, 14, 26   d) 3, 4, 6, 10, 11, 17

   _____   _____

   e) 1, 2, 5, 7, 13, 21, 27, 30   f) 28, 31, 35, 38, 42, 44, 56, 60

   _____   _____

   g) 123, 220, 248, 475, 563   BONUS ▶ 1125, 1253, 1358, 1360, 1454, 1698

   _____   _____

5. Find the highest and lowest value in the stem and leaf plot. Find the range.

a)

Stem	Leaf
2	2 7
3	4 4 6
4	1 7

Highest value: _____

Lowest value: _____

Range: _____ – _____ = _____

b)

Stem	Leaf
0	2 7
1	3 3 4 8
2	0 1 2 4

Highest value: _____

Lowest value: _____

Range: _____ – _____ = _____

c)

Stem	Leaf
8	5 6 7 9
9	0 1 2 2 2 2
10	6

Highest value: _____

Lowest value: _____

Range: _____ – _____ = _____

d)

Stem	Leaf
9	1 2 3 8
10	2 2 3 4 5 5
11	0 1 2

Highest value: _____

Lowest value: _____

Range: _____ – _____ = _____

Neka finds the median from a stem and leaf plot by crossing out the leaves of the highest and lowest values until only one or two leaves remain.

Stem	Leaf
2	5
3	6 7 9
4	3 7

→

Stem	Leaf
2	5̶
3	6 7 9
4	3 7̶

→

Stem	Leaf
2	5̶
3	6̶ ⑦ ⑨
4	3̶ 7̶

The median is halfway between 37 and 39. The median is 38.

6. Find the medians for the stem and leaf plots in Question 5.

a) _____   b) _____   c) _____   d) _____

The **mode** of a data set is the most common data value.
Example: The mode of 3, 7, 3, 9, 4, 7, 4, 4, 5 is 4.

A data set can have more than one mode.
Example: The modes of 2, 2, 3, 3, 3, 4, 4, 4, 5, 5, 6 are 3 and 4.

7. Find the mode or modes of the stem and leaf plots in Question 5.

a) _____   b) _____   c) _____   d) _____

BONUS ▶ a) Give an example of a set of data where the mode

is greater than the median. _____

b) Give an example of a set of data where the mode

is less than the median. _____

PDM4-9 Describing Graphs

1. The graph shows the average number of days of rain or snow each month in Edmonton.

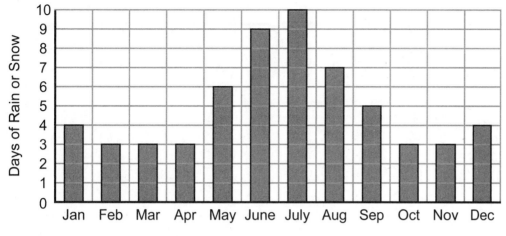

Average Number of Days of Rain or Snow in Edmonton

Month of the Year

a) Fill in the chart from the graph.

Month	Jan	Feb	Mar	Apr	May	June	July	Aug	Sep	Oct	Nov	Dec
Days												

b) Find the range of the data.

_____

c) Find the mode of the data.

_____

d) Find the median of the data.

_____

e) Sally says that you can see from the graph that in most months of the year there are 10 days of rain or snow. Is she correct? Explain.

_____

_____

f) Which season has the most rain or snow? _____

BONUS ▶ Jane says that Edmonton usually has about 3 days of rain or snow per month. David says that Edmonton usually has about 4 days of rain per month. Explain why they are both correct.

_____

_____

2. The graph compares hours of daylight in Iqaluit and Windsor.

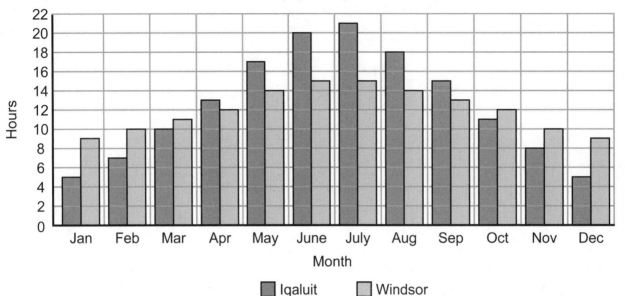

Hours of Daylight in Iqaluit and Windsor

a) Make a stem and leaf plot for the data.

i) Daylight hours in Iqaluit

Stem	Leaf

→

Stem	Leaf

ii) Daylight hours in Windsor

Stem	Leaf

→

Stem	Leaf

b) Find the range in daylight hours in Iqaluit. _____ − _____ = _____

c) Find the range in daylight hours in Windsor. _____ − _____ = _____

d) What is the median number of daylight hours in Iqaluit? _____

e) What is the median number of daylight hours in Windsor? _____

3. Use the graph and your work in Question 2 to answer the question.

a) What is the same about daylight hours in Iqaluit and Windsor and what is different?

_____

_____

b) Name one thing you would like and one thing you wouldn't like about living in Iqaluit and in Windsor.

_____

_____

The area is cut into 4 equal parts.

1 part out of 4 is shaded.

$\frac{1}{4}$ of the area is shaded.

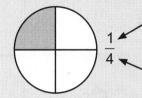

The **numerator** (1) tells you one part is shaded.

The **denominator** (4) tells you how many equal parts are in a whole.

1. Write the fraction shown by the shaded part of the image.

a)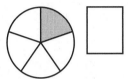

b)

c)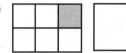

d)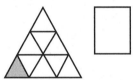

e)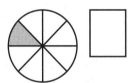

f)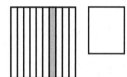

2. Shade the fraction.

a) $\frac{1}{6}$

b) $\frac{1}{5}$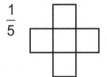

c) $\frac{1}{9}$

d) $\frac{1}{10}$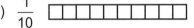

e) $\frac{1}{100}$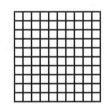

f) $\frac{1}{20}$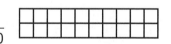

3. Write the words that describe each square in the figure.

one fourth   **one fifth**   **one sixth**   **one seventh**   **one eighth**   **one ninth**

a)

b)

c)

_____   _____   _____

4. Write the fraction shown by the shaded part of the figure.

a)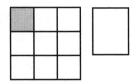

b)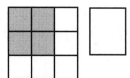

c)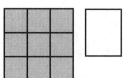

d)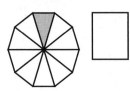

e)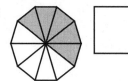

f)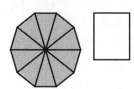

5. Shade the fraction.

a) $\dfrac{1}{7}$

b) $\dfrac{3}{7}$

c) $\dfrac{6}{7}$

d) $\dfrac{1}{8}$

e) $\dfrac{5}{8}$

f) $\dfrac{7}{8}$

6. Find a fraction in the top row that is equal to a fraction in the bottom row.
Fill in the blank with the letter from the fraction in the top row.

A.   B.   C.   D.

a)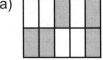

b)

c)

d)

_____   _____   _____   _____

7. Shade the fraction twice. Put a ✔ under the figure with the larger amount of shading.

a) $\dfrac{1}{10}$

b) $\dfrac{4}{10}$

c) $\dfrac{7}{10}$

☐   ☐   ☐   ☐   ☐   ☐

1. Shade half of the figure. Write two fractions to describe the shaded part.

a) 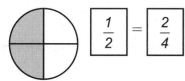 $\dfrac{1}{2} = \dfrac{2}{4}$

b)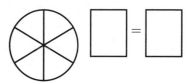

c)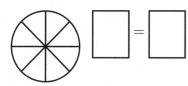

d)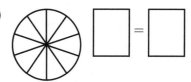

2. Circle the fractions that are more than half.

$\dfrac{3}{4}$ $\dfrac{3}{5}$ $\dfrac{3}{6}$ $\dfrac{3}{7}$ $\dfrac{3}{8}$

Is $\dfrac{3}{5}$ more than $\dfrac{1}{2}$ or less than $\dfrac{1}{2}$?

There are 5 parts altogether. $5 - 3 = 2$ parts are not shaded.

When more parts are shaded than not shaded, the fraction is greater than $\dfrac{1}{2}$, so $\dfrac{3}{5} > \dfrac{1}{2}$.

---

3. How many shaded parts does the fraction show? How many parts are not shaded?

a) _____ shaded

_____ not shaded

b) _____ shaded

_____ not shaded

c) _____ shaded

_____ not shaded

4. Write > or <.

a) $\dfrac{2}{5} \square \dfrac{1}{2}$ b) $\dfrac{4}{9} \square \dfrac{1}{2}$ c) $\dfrac{6}{11} \square \dfrac{1}{2}$ d) $\dfrac{13}{25} \square \dfrac{1}{2}$ e) $\dfrac{23}{50} \square \dfrac{1}{2}$ f) $\dfrac{5}{11} \square \dfrac{1}{2}$

5. Karen drank $\dfrac{3}{8}$ of a bottle of milk. Ella drank $\dfrac{6}{11}$ of it. Who drank more milk?

Hint: Compare the fractions to $\dfrac{1}{2}$. _____

6. Glen ran around $\dfrac{3}{5}$ of a track. Yu ran around $\dfrac{1}{3}$ of it. Who ran farther? _____

Rob really likes pizza! The pizza has 4 slices, and Rob ate 4 slices:

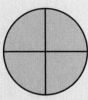 Rob ate $\frac{4}{4}$ of a pizza. Rob ate 1 pizza.

7. Write the shaded fraction.

a)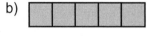

b)

c)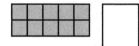

8. A fraction is equal to 1 if its numerator and denominator are _____.

Rob does not like this pizza at all! The pizza has 4 slices, and Rob ate 0 slices:

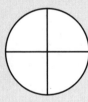 Rob ate $\frac{0}{4}$ of a pizza. Rob ate none of the pizza.

9. Write if the fraction is "equal to" or "greater than" 0.

a) The fraction is _____ 0.   b) The fraction is _____ 0.

10. A fraction is equal to 0 if its numerator is _____.

11. Shade two different fractions between 0 and $\frac{1}{2}$, and then write the fractions.

 This fraction is ☐ .

This fraction is ☐ .

12. Shade two different fractions between $\frac{1}{2}$ and 1, and then write the fractions.

 This fraction is ☐ .

This fraction is ☐ .

NS4-47 Equivalent Fractions

1. How many times as many parts are there?

a) has _____ times as many parts as .

b) has _____ times as many parts as .

c) has _____ times as many parts as .

d) has _____ times as many parts as .

2. Fill in the blanks.

a) A has _____ times as many parts as B.

   A has _____ times as many shaded parts as B.

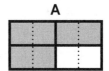 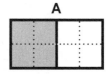 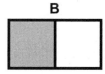

b) A has _____ times as many parts as B.

   A has _____ times as many shaded parts as B.

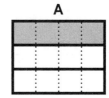 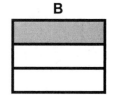

c) A has _____ times as many parts as B.

   A has _____ times as many shaded parts as B.

d) A has _____ times as many parts as B.

   A has _____ times as many shaded parts as B.

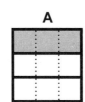

3. The picture shows two equivalent fractions. Fill in the blanks.

a) $\dfrac{1}{5}$ and $\dfrac{2}{10}$

2 is _____ times as much as 1.

10 is _____ times as much as 5.

b)  $\dfrac{4}{5}$ and $\dfrac{12}{15}$

12 is _____ times as much as 4.

15 is _____ times as much as 5.

c) 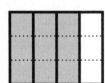 $\dfrac{1}{4}$ and $\dfrac{2}{8}$

2 is _____ times as much as 1.

8 is _____ times as much as 4.

d) 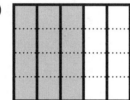 $\dfrac{3}{5}$ and $\dfrac{12}{20}$

12 is _____ times as much as 3.

20 is _____ times as much as 5.

4. Write an equivalent fraction for the picture. Then write how many times as much the new numerator and denominator are.

a) 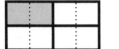 $\dfrac{3}{4} = \boxed{\dfrac{9}{12}}$

  _3_ times as much

b) 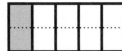 $\dfrac{1}{4} = \boxed{}$

  _____ times as much

c) 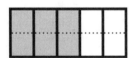 $\dfrac{3}{5} = \boxed{}$

  _____ times as much

BONUS ▶

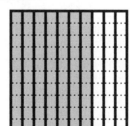 $\dfrac{7}{10} = \boxed{}$

  _____ times as much

To get an equivalent fraction, multiply the numerator **and** denominator by the same number.

Example: Picture A   Picture B

    $\dfrac{3}{4} \xrightarrow[\times 2]{\times 2} \dfrac{6}{8}$

Picture B has twice as many **parts** as Picture A.
Picture B has twice as many **shaded parts** as Picture A.

5. Draw lines to cut the pies into more equal pieces. Then fill in the numerators of the equivalent fractions.

a)

4 pieces   6 pieces   8 pieces

$\dfrac{1}{2} = \dfrac{}{4} = \dfrac{}{6} = \dfrac{}{8}$

b)

6 pieces   9 pieces   12 pieces

$\dfrac{1}{3} = \dfrac{}{6} = \dfrac{}{9} = \dfrac{}{12}$

6. Draw lines to cut the pie into more pieces. Then fill in the missing numbers.

a)

    $\dfrac{2}{3} \xrightarrow[\times 2]{\times 2} \dfrac{}{6}$

b)

     $\dfrac{3}{4} \xrightarrow[\times]{\times} \dfrac{}{8}$

c)

    $\dfrac{2}{3} \xrightarrow[\times]{\times} \dfrac{}{9}$

↖ This number tells you how many pieces to cut each slice into.

7. Use multiplication to find the equivalent fraction.

a) $\dfrac{1 \times 2}{3 \times 2} = \dfrac{}{6}$

b) $\dfrac{1 \times}{2 \times} = \dfrac{}{10}$

c) $\dfrac{2}{5} = \dfrac{}{10}$

d) $\dfrac{3}{4} = \dfrac{}{8}$

e) $\dfrac{1}{4} = \dfrac{}{12}$

f) $\dfrac{4}{5} = \dfrac{}{15}$

g) $\dfrac{5}{6} = \dfrac{}{12}$

h) $\dfrac{3}{10} = \dfrac{}{100}$

i) $\dfrac{5}{9} = \dfrac{}{72}$

8. Write five fractions equivalent to $\dfrac{2}{3}$.

$\dfrac{2}{3} = \boxed{} = \boxed{} = \boxed{} = \boxed{} = \boxed{}$

NS4-48 Comparing and Ordering Fractions

1. a) Write the numerators of the shaded fractions.

$$\frac{}{4} \qquad\qquad \frac{}{4} \qquad\qquad \frac{}{4}$$

   b) Look at the pictures and fractions in part a) from left to right.
   Write "increases," "decreases," or "stays the same."

   i) Numerator _____.

   ii) Denominator _____.

   iii) Shaded fraction _____.

Comparing fractions when ...

the numerator changes   **and**   **the denominator stays the same**

$$\frac{1}{5}$$

fewer shaded parts →   ← same number and size of parts

more shaded parts →   ←

$$\frac{2}{5}$$

So $\frac{2}{5} > \frac{1}{5}$ because more parts are shaded.

---

2. Circle the greater fraction.

   a) $\frac{2}{5}$ or $\frac{4}{5}$ b) $\frac{3}{4}$ or $\frac{1}{4}$ c) $\frac{4}{10}$ or $\frac{9}{10}$ d) $\frac{3}{3}$ or $\frac{1}{3}$

3. Write any number in the blank that makes the relationship correct.

   a) $\frac{3}{7} > \frac{1}{7}$ b) $\frac{}{29} < \frac{14}{29}$ c) $\frac{61}{385} > \frac{}{385}$ **BONUS ▶** $\frac{}{1000} < \frac{2}{1000}$

4. Two fractions have the same denominator but different numerators.
   How can you tell which fraction is greater?

   _____

   _____

5. Use the number line to order the fractions from least to greatest.

Draw an ✘ to mark the position of each fraction.

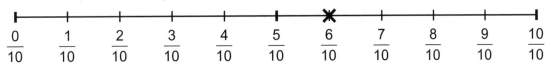

$$\frac{0}{10} \quad \frac{1}{10} \quad \frac{2}{10} \quad \frac{3}{10} \quad \frac{4}{10} \quad \frac{5}{10} \quad \frac{6}{10} \quad \frac{7}{10} \quad \frac{8}{10} \quad \frac{9}{10} \quad \frac{10}{10}$$

$$\frac{6}{10} \quad \frac{1}{10} \quad \frac{8}{10} \quad \frac{4}{10} \quad \frac{2}{10} \quad \frac{9}{10} \quad \frac{5}{10}$$

☐ < ☐ < ☐ < ☐ < ☐ < ☐ < ☐

6. Order the fractions from least to greatest by considering the numerators and denominators.

a) $\frac{3}{5} \quad \frac{0}{5} \quad \frac{2}{5} \quad \frac{5}{5} \quad \frac{1}{5}$

☐ < ☐ < ☐ < ☐ < ☐

b) $\frac{6}{10} \quad \frac{1}{10} \quad \frac{4}{10} \quad \frac{2}{10} \quad \frac{9}{10}$

☐ < ☐ < ☐ < ☐ < ☐

7. a) What fraction of a litre is in the container?

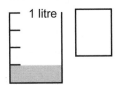

b) Which fraction in part a) is ...

    i) the smallest? ☐   ii) the biggest? ☐   iii) in the middle? ☐

c) Write "smaller" or "bigger." As the denominator gets bigger, each part gets _____.

Comparing fractions when ...

the numerator stays the same   and   **the denominator changes**

$$\frac{1}{5}$$

same number of shaded parts ← smaller parts

← bigger parts

$$\frac{1}{3}$$

So $\frac{1}{5} < \frac{1}{3}$ because the parts are smaller in the shape with more parts.

---

8. Circle the greater fraction.

a) $\dfrac{2}{5}$ or $\dfrac{2}{3}$

b) $\dfrac{3}{4}$ or $\dfrac{3}{5}$

c) $\dfrac{4}{5}$ or $\dfrac{4}{10}$

d) $\dfrac{3}{4}$ or $\dfrac{3}{3}$

9. Write any number in the blank that makes the relationship correct.

a) $\dfrac{3}{5} > \dfrac{}{8}$

b) $\dfrac{}{15} > \dfrac{14}{29}$

c) $\dfrac{9}{16} > \dfrac{9}{}$

d) $\dfrac{20}{} < \dfrac{20}{27}$

10. Two fractions have the same numerator but different denominators.
How can you tell which fraction is greater?

_____

_____

11. a) Order the fractions from least to greatest by matching each fraction to the strip
it represents and then shading it.

i) $\dfrac{1}{4}\ \ \dfrac{1}{10}\ \ \dfrac{1}{2}\ \ \dfrac{1}{5}\ \ \dfrac{1}{3}$
ii) $\dfrac{2}{2}\ \ \dfrac{2}{4}\ \ \dfrac{2}{10}\ \ \dfrac{2}{3}\ \ \dfrac{2}{5}$

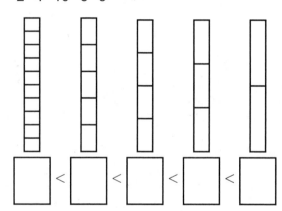

b) Order the fractions from least to greatest by considering the numerators and denominators.

i) $\dfrac{1}{4}\ \ \dfrac{1}{10}\ \ \dfrac{1}{2}\ \ \dfrac{1}{5}\ \ \dfrac{1}{3}$
ii) $\dfrac{2}{2}\ \ \dfrac{2}{4}\ \ \dfrac{2}{10}\ \ \dfrac{2}{3}\ \ \dfrac{2}{5}$

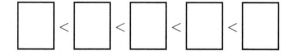

c) Are your answers for parts a) and b) the same? Explain.

_____

_____

12. Randi says that $\frac{1}{2}$ of a pie is less than $\frac{1}{10}$ of a pie. Is she correct? Explain.

_____

_____

13. Ray, Hanna, and Lynn each brought 1 cake to school for their year-end class party. None of the cakes are the same size. The teacher cut each cake into 8 equal pieces, so everyone in the class can have a piece. Ray says, "That's not fair at all!" and Lynn says, "That's perfectly fair!"

a) Why does Ray think it's unfair?

_____

_____

b) Why does Lynn think it's fair?

_____

_____

14. a) Write the fractions in the correct category.

$\frac{3}{4}$ $\frac{1}{3}$ $\frac{2}{5}$ $\frac{4}{6}$

$\frac{4}{9}$ $\frac{3}{7}$ $\frac{7}{8}$ $\frac{6}{10}$

$\frac{5}{9}$ $\frac{2}{3}$ $\frac{1}{6}$ $\frac{3}{10}$

0 to $\frac{1}{2}$	$\frac{1}{2}$ to 1
	$\frac{3}{4}$

b) Use the results from part a) to write "<" or ">" in the box between the pair of fractions.

i) $\frac{6}{10}$ ☐ $\frac{3}{7}$ ii) $\frac{1}{3}$ ☐ $\frac{3}{4}$ iii) $\frac{4}{6}$ ☐ $\frac{4}{9}$ iv) $\frac{2}{5}$ ☐ $\frac{5}{9}$

v) $\frac{2}{3}$ ☐ $\frac{3}{10}$ vi) $\frac{3}{7}$ ☐ $\frac{7}{8}$ vii) $\frac{5}{9}$ ☐ $\frac{1}{6}$ viii) $\frac{4}{9}$ ☐ $\frac{3}{4}$

NS4-49 Equal Parts of a Set

Fractions can name parts of a set:

$\frac{1}{5}$ of the figures are squares, $\frac{1}{5}$ are circles, and $\frac{3}{5}$ are triangles.

1. Write fractions in the blanks.

   a) ⬤ △ ◯

   ☐ of the figures are circles.

   ☐ of the figures are shaded.

   b) ▨ ▨ ☐ ⬤ △

   ☐ of the figures are shaded.

   ☐ of the figures are triangles.

2. ▨ △ △ ⬤ ☐ ☐ ▲ ☐

   a) $\frac{5}{8}$ of the figures are _____ .

   b) $\frac{3}{8}$ of the figures are _____ .

3. A soccer team wins 5 games and loses 3 games.

   a) How many games did the team play? _____

   b) What fraction of the games did the team win? ☐

4. A box contains 4 blue markers, 3 black markers, and 3 red markers.
   What fraction of the markers are **not** blue? You can make a picture to help.

5. Write four fraction statements for the picture:

6. Draw a picture that fits all the clues.

   a) There are 5 circles and squares.

      $\frac{3}{5}$ of the figures are squares.

      $\frac{2}{5}$ of the figures are shaded.

      Two circles are shaded.

   b) There are 5 triangles and squares.

      $\frac{3}{5}$ of the figures are shaded.

      $\frac{2}{5}$ of the figures are triangles.

      One square is shaded.

NS4-50 Fractions of Whole Numbers

Don has 6 cookies.

He wants to give $\frac{1}{3}$ of his cookies to a friend.

He makes 3 equal groups and gives 1 group to his friend.

There are 2 cookies in each group, so $\frac{1}{3}$ of 6 is 2.

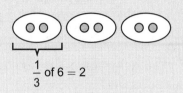

$\frac{1}{3}$ of 6 = 2

1. Use the picture to find the fraction of the number.

a)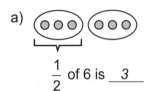

$\frac{1}{2}$ of 6 is ___3___

b)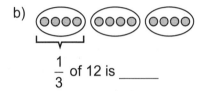

$\frac{1}{3}$ of 12 is _____

c)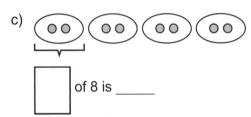

☐ of 8 is _____

d)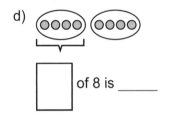

☐ of 8 is _____

Tina has 10 cookies. She wants to give $\frac{3}{5}$ of her cookies to a friend. She makes 5 equal groups and gives 3 of the groups to her friend.

There are 2 in each group. So there are 6 in 3 groups. So $\frac{3}{5}$ of 10 is 6.

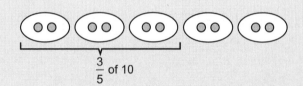

$\frac{3}{5}$ of 10

2. Circle the given amount.

a) $\frac{2}{3}$ of 6

b) $\frac{3}{4}$ of 8

c) $\frac{4}{5}$ of 10

d) $\frac{3}{4}$ of 12

3. Draw the correct number of dots in each group, and then circle the given amount.

a) $\frac{2}{3}$ of 12

b) $\frac{2}{3}$ of 9

4. Draw a picture to find $\frac{3}{4}$ of 12 cookies.

Tristan finds $\frac{1}{3}$ of 6 by dividing: 6 divided into 3 equal groups is 2 in each group.

 $6 \div 3 = 2$ So $\frac{1}{3}$ of 6 is 2.

5. Find the fraction of the number. Write the division you used in the box.

a) $\frac{1}{2}$ of 8 = ___4___   b) $\frac{1}{2}$ of 10 = _____   c) $\frac{1}{2}$ of 16 = _____   d) $\frac{1}{2}$ of 20 = _____

$8 \div 2$

e) $\frac{1}{3}$ of 9 = _____   f) $\frac{1}{3}$ of 15 = _____   **BONUS▶** $\frac{1}{1000}$ of 4000 = _____

6. Circle $\frac{1}{2}$ of the set of lines. Hint: Count the lines and divide by 2.

a) | | | | | |

b) | | | | | | | | |

c) | | | | | | | | | | | |

d) | | | | | | | | | | | | | |

7. Shade $\frac{1}{3}$ of the circles. Then circle $\frac{2}{3}$.

a)

b) ○○○○○○○○○○○○

c) ○○○

d) ○○○○○○○
○○○○○○

8. Shade $\frac{1}{4}$ of the triangles. Then circle $\frac{3}{4}$.

9. Shade $\frac{3}{5}$ of the boxes. Hint: First count the boxes and find $\frac{1}{5}$.

a)

b)

Ansel finds $\frac{2}{3}$ of 12 as follows:

Step 1: He finds $\frac{1}{3}$ of 12 by dividing 12 by 3:

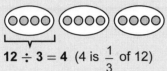

$12 \div 3 = 4$ (4 is $\frac{1}{3}$ of 12)

Step 2: He multiplies the result by 2:

$4 \times 2 = 8$ (8 is $\frac{2}{3}$ of 12)

10. Find the amount using Ansel's method.

a) $\frac{2}{3}$ of 9

$\frac{1}{3}$ of 9 is _____

So $\frac{2}{3}$ of 9 is _____.

b) $\frac{3}{4}$ of 8

$\frac{1}{4}$ of 8 is _____

So $\frac{3}{4}$ of 8 is _____.

c) $\frac{2}{3}$ of 15

$\frac{1}{3}$ of 15 is _____

So $\frac{2}{3}$ of 15 is _____.

d) $\frac{2}{5}$ of 10

$\frac{1}{5}$ of 10 is _____

So $\frac{2}{5}$ of 10 is _____.

e) $\frac{3}{5}$ of 25

_____

f) $\frac{2}{7}$ of 14

_____

g) $\frac{1}{6}$ of 18

_____

h) $\frac{1}{2}$ of 12

_____

i) $\frac{3}{4}$ of 12

_____

j) $\frac{2}{3}$ of 21

_____

k) $\frac{3}{8}$ of 16

_____

l) $\frac{3}{7}$ of 21

_____

11. Five children are on a bus. $\frac{3}{5}$ are girls. How many girls are on the bus? _____

12. One kilogram of plums costs $8. How much would $\frac{3}{4}$ of a kilogram cost? _____

13. Josh has 12 apples. He gave away $\frac{3}{4}$ of the apples. How many did he keep? _____

BONUS▶ Karen has 120 stamps. She gave away $\frac{3}{4}$ of the stamps.

How many did she keep? _____

NS4-51 Fraction Word Problems

1. $\frac{5}{9}$ of the community pool is reserved for swimming lengths. What fraction of the pool

    is not reserved for swimming lengths? ☐

2. A pitcher of fruit drink is made by mixing water and canned orange juice.

    a) If $\frac{1}{4}$ of the fruit drink is canned orange juice, what fraction of the drink is water? ☐

    b) How would the taste of the fruit drink change if $\frac{1}{2}$ of it were canned orange juice instead of $\frac{1}{4}$?

    _____

    c) If you added some club soda to a glass of fruit drink, would the fraction of canned juice in the glass
       of fruit drink get bigger or smaller? Explain.

    _____

    _____

3. The picture represents a set of stickers.

    a) What are two examples of $\frac{4}{9}$ of the stickers? _____

    b) What fraction of the stickers are quadrilaterals (have exactly four sides)? ☐

    c) What fraction of the quadrilaterals do not have four equal sides? ☐

    d) What other group can be represented with the same fraction as in c)?

    _____

4. The picture represents the fraction of Earth's surface that is covered by water.

    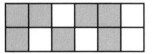

    a) What fraction of Earth's surface is covered by water (shaded)? ☐

    b) What fraction of Earth's surface is not covered by water? ☐

    c) Which is there more of, Earth's surface with water or without water? _____

5. Lela and Ray went to the park. The pictures represent the fraction of time each spent on the swings.

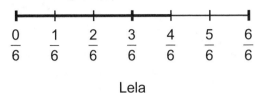   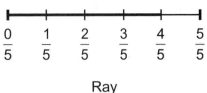

Lela   Ray

a) What fraction of the time at the park did Lela spend on the swings? ☐

b) What fraction of the time at the park did Ray spend on the swings? ☐

c) Who spent more time on the swings? _____

6. A teacher is going to order 10 pizzas for a year-end party. More than half of the pizzas must be vegetarian.

a) Will there be enough vegetarian pizzas if 3 are vegetarian? _____

b) Will there be enough vegetarian pizzas if 6 are vegetarian? _____

c) If 6 pizzas are vegetarian, what fraction of the pizzas are not vegetarian? ☐

d) Give another example of a fraction that would have enough vegetarian pizzas by shading the pizzas below.

7. Soccer Team A won $\frac{3}{9}$ of the games they played this season. Soccer Team B lost $\frac{5}{9}$ of the games they played this season. Soccer Team C won $\frac{3}{5}$ of the games they played this season.

a) What fraction of their games did Team A lose? ☐

b) What fraction of their games did Team B win? ☐

c) What fraction of their games did Team C lose? ☐

d) Which team won a greater fraction of their games, Team A or Team B? _____

e) Which team won a greater fraction of their games, Team A or Team C? _____

NS4-52 Decimal Tenths and Place Value

A **tenth** (or $\frac{1}{10}$) can be represented in different ways.

A tenth of the distance
between 0 and 1

A tenth of a pie

A tenth of a
square

Mathematicians invented decimal tenths as a short form for tenths: $\frac{1}{10} = 0.1$, $\frac{2}{10} = 0.2$, and so on.

1. Write a fraction and a decimal for the shaded part in the boxes.

a) $\frac{4}{10}$ 0.4

b)

c)

2. Write the decimal.

a) 5 tenths = __0.5__   b) 7 tenths = _____   c) 6 tenths = _____   d) 9 tenths = _____

e) 2 tenths = _____   f) 8 tenths = _____   g) 3 tenths = _____

BONUS ▶ 0 tenths = _____

3. Shade to show the decimal.

a) 0.3

b) 0.8

c) 0.5

d) 0.6

4. Show the decimal on the number line.

a) 0.8 of the distance from 0.0 to 1.0

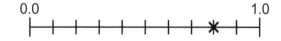

b) 0.3 of the distance from 0.0 to 1.0

c) 0.5 of the distance from 0.0 to 1.0

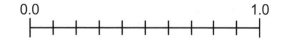

d) 0.9 of the distance from 0.0 to 1.0

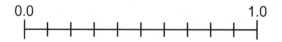

4375.6

thousands
hundreds
tens
ones
decimal point
tenths

5. Write the place value of the underlined digit.

a) 2.7 _____ones_____

b) 53.9 _____

c) 107.1 _____

d) 236.4 _____

e) 4501.8 _____

f) 7334.5 _____

g) 400.3 _____

h) 921.2 _____

i) 3677.8 _____

6. Write the place value of the digit 3 in the number.
Hint: First underline the 3 in the number.

a) 2361.9 _____

b) 405.3 _____

c) 713.8 _____

d) 30.2 _____

e) 3919.1 _____

f) 2854.3 _____

g) 392.7 _____

h) 1636.2 _____

i) 3544.5 _____

You can also write numbers using a place value chart. Example:

This is the number 7102.8 in a place value chart:

Thousands	Hundreds	Tens	Ones	Tenths
7	1	0	2	8

7. Write the number into the place value chart.

		Thousands	Hundreds	Tens	Ones	Tenths
a)	5227.6	5	2	2	7	6
b)	8053.4					
c)	489.2					
d)	27.8					
e)	9104.5					
f)	8.7					
g)	706.0					
h)	6.1					

In the number 2836.5:

the **digit** 2 has a value of 2000—the **value** of the digit 2 is 2000;

the digit 8 has a value of 800—the value of the digit 8 is 800;

the digit 3 has a value of 30—the value of the digit 3 is 30;

the digit 6 has a value of 6—the value of the digit 6 is 6; and

the digit 5 has a value of $\frac{5}{10}$ —the value of the digit 5 is $\frac{5}{10}$.

8. Write the value of each digit.

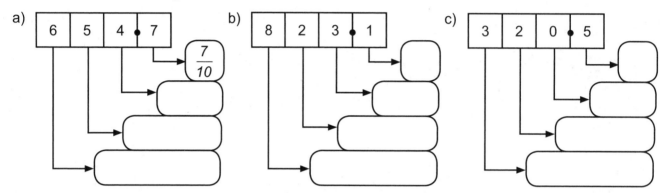

9. What value does the digit 7 have in the number?

a) 732.6

| 700 |

b) 4107.9

c) 6171.2

d) 7384.5

e) 9062.7

f) 467.8

g) 1894.7

h) 2744.8

i) 7250.5

j) 6000.7

k) 3975.4

l) 743.1

10. Fill in the blank.

a) In the number 1969.5, the digit 6 stands for ___60___.

b) In the number 5873.2, the digit 3 stands for _____.

c) In the number 7451.3, the value of the digit 7 is _____.

d) In the number 8003.9, the value of the digit 9 is _____.

e) In the number 4855.7, the value of the digit 8 is _____.

f) In the number 9201.4, the digit _____ is in the ones place.

g) In the number 3495.6, the digit _____ is in the hundreds place.

h) In the number 6467.5, the digit _____ is in the tenths place.

1. a) Write a fraction in each blank above the number line.

    b) Write a decimal in each blank below the number line.

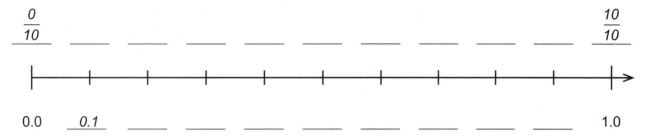

    c) Which decimal is equal to the fraction?

    i) $\dfrac{5}{10}$ = _____

    ii) $\dfrac{10}{10}$ = _____

    iii) $\dfrac{0}{10}$ = _____

2. a) Write a decimal in each blank below the number line.

    b) Cross out each incorrect fraction and write the correct fraction above it.

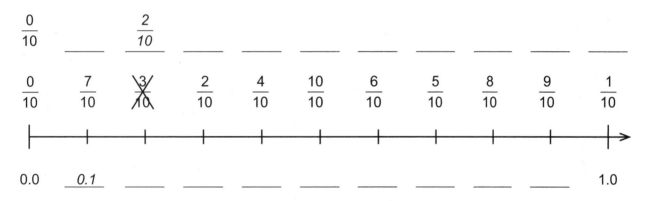

3. a) Write a fraction in each blank above the number line.

    b) Cross out each incorrect decimal on the number line and write the correct decimal below it.

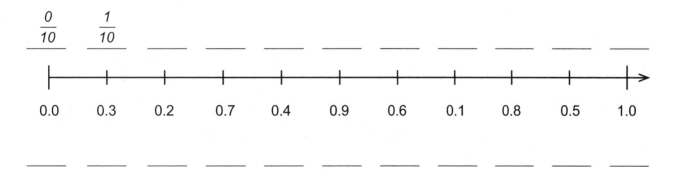

4. **a)** Fill in the missing numerators and decimals on the number lines.

$$\frac{0}{2}$$ ____ $$\frac{\ \ }{2}$$ ____ $$\frac{\ \ }{2}$$ ____

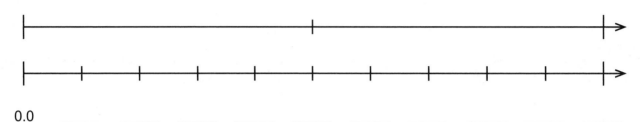

0.0   ____   ____   ____   ____   ____   ____   ____   ____   ____

    b) Write the decimal that the fraction is equal to.

      i) $\dfrac{0}{2}$ = _0.0_   **ii)** $\dfrac{1}{2}$ = _____   **iii)** $\dfrac{2}{2}$ = _____

    BONUS ▶ Write the decimals that are not equal to any fraction in part b).

     _0.1_   _0.2_   ____   ____   ____   ____   ____   ____

5. **a)** Fill in the missing fractions and decimals.

$$\frac{0}{5}$$ ____   ____   ____   ____   ____

0.0   ____   ____   ____   ____   ____   ____   ____   ____   ____

    b) Write the decimal the fraction is equal to in part b).

      i) $\dfrac{4}{5}$ = _____   **ii)** $\dfrac{2}{5}$ = _____   **iii)** $\dfrac{5}{5}$ = _____

      iv) $\dfrac{1}{5}$ = _____   **v)** $\dfrac{0}{5}$ = _____

    BONUS ▶ Write the decimals that are not equal to any fraction in part b).

     _0.1_   _0.3_   ____   ____   ____   ____

NS4-54 Decimals Greater Than 1—to Tenths

1. Write a decimal in each blank below the number line.

a)

1.0   _1.1_   _____   _____   _____   _____   _____   _____   _____   _____   2.0

b)
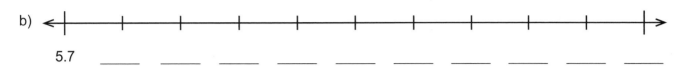

5.7   _____   _____   _____   _____   _____   _____   _____   _____   _____   _____

c)

63.4   _____   _____   _____   _____   _____   _____   _____   _____   _____   _____

2. a) How are the scales in Question 1 different from each other?

_____

_____

b) How are the scales in Question 1 the same as each other?

_____

_____

> You can write a decimal in words. Use "and" for the decimal point.
>
> Examples: 12.3 = twelve **and** three tenths   2.8 = two **and** eight tenths

3. Fill in the missing number word.

a) 3.1 = three and _____*one*_____ tenth

b) 18.7 = eighteen and _____ tenths

c) 6.5 = _____ and five tenths

d) 20.8 = _____ and eight tenths

4. Write the equivalent words or decimal.

a) 7.4 = _____

b) 4.9 = _____

c) nineteen and one tenth = _____

d) sixty-two and four tenths = _____

5. Count the shaded tenths. Write the amount two ways.

a)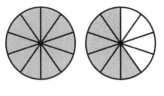

___16___ tenths = ___1.6___

b)

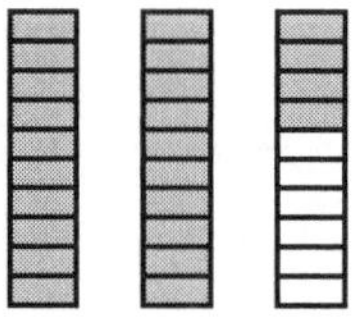

_____ tenths = _____

c)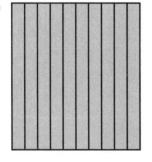

_____ tenths = _____

d)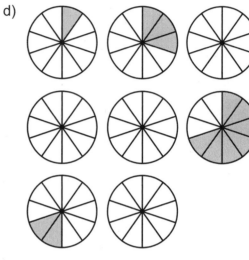

_____ tenths = _____

e)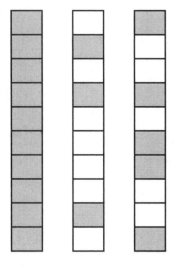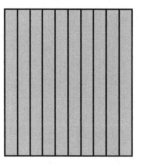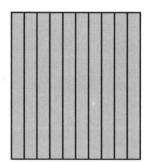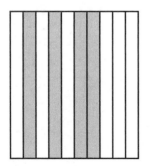

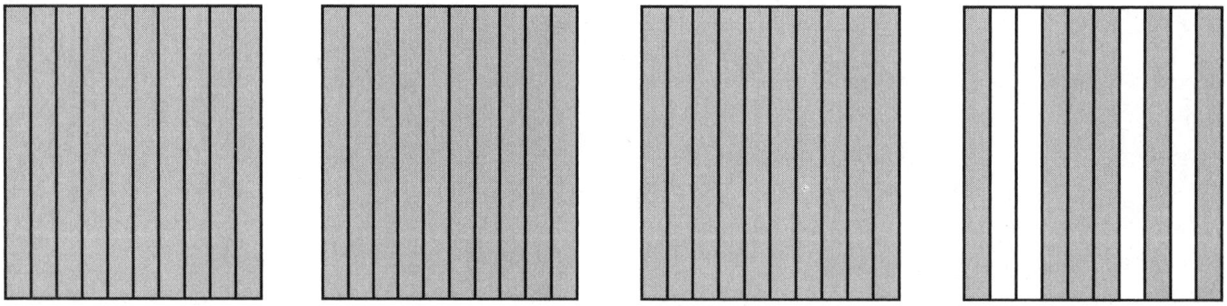

_____ tenths = _____

BONUS ▶

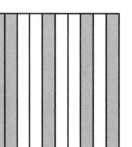 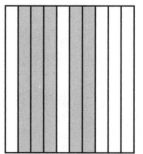

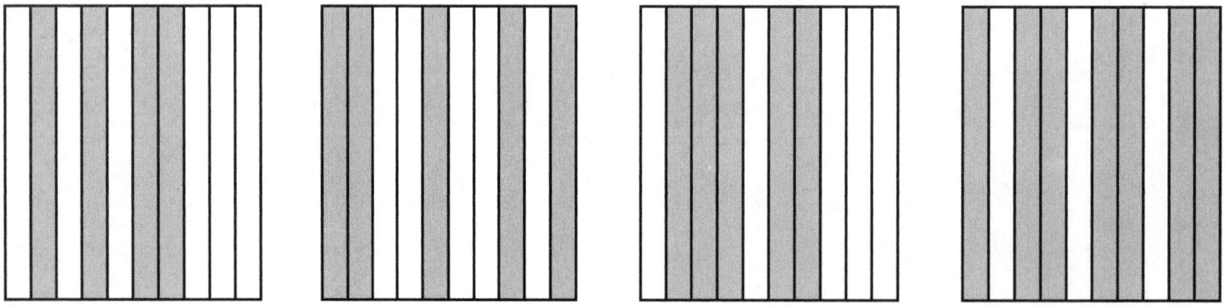

_____ tenths = _____

□ = 1   ▯ = 0.1

1. Write the number for each base ten model using numerals (in the box).
   Then circle the greater number in the pair.

   a) 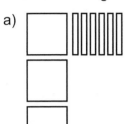   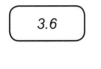 3.6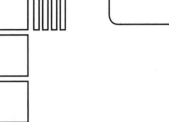

   b)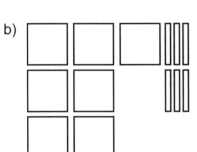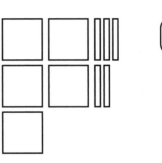

   c) Explain how you knew which number in part a) was greater.

2. Draw base ten models for the pair of numbers. Then circle the greater number.

   a) nine and seven tenths   7.9

   b) twelve and eight tenths   8.2

3. Write the value of each digit. Then complete the sentence.

a) 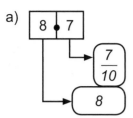　　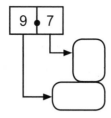

b) 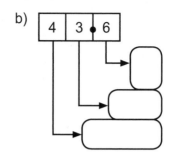　　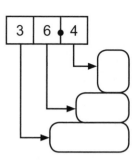

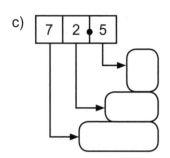

_____ is greater than _____ .　　　_____ is greater than _____ .

c) 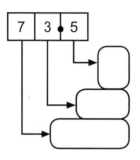　　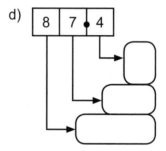　　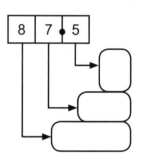

d)

_____ is greater than _____ .　　　_____ is greater than _____ .

4. Circle the digits that are different in the pair of numbers. Then write the greater number in the box.

a) 24⦶.5
246.5

| 247.5 |

b) 136.0
126.0

| |

c) 4852.5
4858.5

| |

d) 632.5
732.5

| |

5. Read the numbers from left to right. Circle the first pair of digits you find that are different. Then write the greater number in the box.

a) 43⦶3.3
43⦶2.3

| |

b) 5090.7
5900.7

| |

c) 756.2
776.8

| |

BONUS ▶ 12 146.6
12 086.4

| |

6. Circle the greater number.

a) 8147.6　　9147.6

b) 352.1　　325.9

c) 5098.1　　5089.9

7. Write "<" (less than) or ">" (greater than) in the box to make the statement true.

a) 6726.2 ▢ 6726.6

b) 788.8 ▢ 788.7

c) 4303.2 ▢ 3403.9

8. Write the second number below the first number with the decimal points lined up.
Then circle the greater number.

a) (1296.8)   689.8   b) 416.2   96.2   c) 5137.2   5371.2   d) 7358.2   735.8

___689.8___   _____   _____   _____

9. Circle the greatest number.

a) 68.1   86.1   81.6   b) 98.3   109.3   319.4

c) 3670.1   3063.7   736.6   d) 5228.2   2558.2   852.8

10. Arrange the numbers in descending order.

a) 549.1   5490.1   954.1   b) 1300.4   10 002.4   989.7

_____, _____, _____   _____, _____, _____

c) 826.7   762.8   800.0   d) 400.1   1000.4   410.0

_____, _____, _____   _____, _____, _____

11. Write a number in each blank so the three numbers are arranged in ascending order.

a) 529.9, _____, 592.2   b) 614.4, 641.1, _____   c) _____, 79.3, 790.3

_____, 529.9, 592.2   614.4, _____, 641.1   79.3, 790.3, _____

529.9, 592.2, _____   _____, 614.4, 641.1   79.3, _____, 790.3

12. a) Mark the numbers on the number line using an ✘. Then write the numbers in ascending
and descending order: 519.7, 519.3, 520.0.

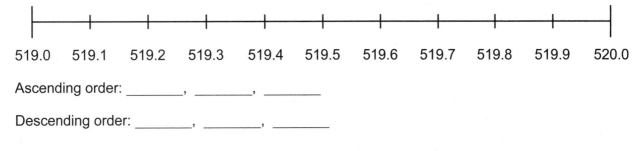

519.0   519.1   519.2   519.3   519.4   519.5   519.6   519.7   519.8   519.9   520.0

Ascending order: _____, _____, _____

Descending order: _____, _____, _____

b) Explain why it would be difficult to make a number line to mark the numbers 43.9, 9432.2,
and 432.9 on.

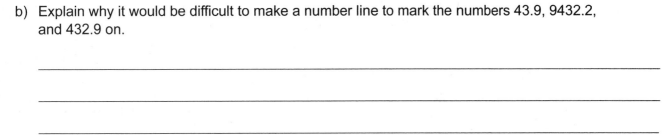

_____

_____

_____

Number Sense 4-55

NS4-56 Adding and Subtracting Decimals—to Tenths

A base ten representation for decimal tenths:

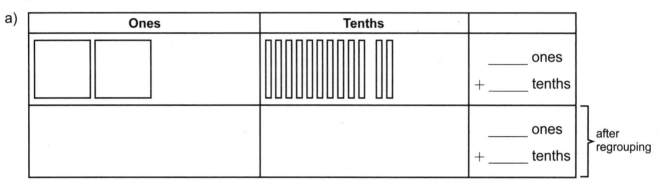

1 one   1 tenth   1 one   =   10 tenths

1. Regroup every 10 tenths as 1 one.

a)

Ones	Tenths	
[two squares]	[eleven tenths + 2 tenths]	_____ ones + _____ tenths
		_____ ones + _____ tenths } after regrouping

b) 16 tenths = _____ ones + _____ tenths   c) 23 tenths = _____ ones + _____ tenths

d) 49 tenths = _____ ones + _____ tenths   e) 52 tenths = _____ ones + _____ tenths

2. Regroup so that the tenths place value has a single digit.

a) 3 tenths + 12 tenths = ___1___ one + ___5___ tenths

b) 7 ones + 14 tenths = _____ ones + _____ tenths

c) 8 tens + 6 ones + 36 tenths = _____ tens + _____ ones + _____ tenths

d) 6 hundreds + 5 tens + 4 ones + 54 tenths = _____ hundreds + _____ tens + _____ ones
    + _____ tenths

BONUS ▶ 9 thousands + 3 hundreds + 7 tens + 2 ones + 28 tenths = _____ thousands
    + _____ hundreds + _____ tens + _____ ones + _____ tenths

3. Add by adding each place value.

a) 35.4 + 2.3

	Tens	Ones	Tenths
	3	5	4
+		2	3
	3	7	7

b) 146.1 + 22.8

	Hundreds	Tens	Ones	Tenths
+				

4. Add by adding each place value. Then regroup.

a) 14.5 + 3.6

	Tens	Ones	Tenths
	1	4	5
+		3	6
	1	7	11
	1	8	1

← after regrouping →

b) 25.8 + 12.6

	Tens	Ones	Tenths
+			

5. Add the decimals by lining up the decimal points.

a) 6.5 + 3.2

b) 11.3 + 32.5

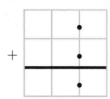

c) 65.6 + 2.3

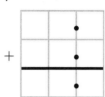

d) 37.2 + 42.6

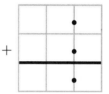

You can show regrouping on a grid. Example: 4.8 + 3.5

	1	
	4	8
+	3	5
	8	3

8 tenths + 5 tenths = 13 tenths were regrouped as **1** one and **3** tenths

6. Add the decimals by lining up the decimal points. You will need to regroup.

a) 6.7 + 1.8

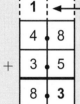

	1	
	6	7
+	1	8
	8	5

b) 24.7 + 4.3

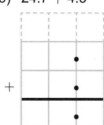

c) 57.2 + 31.9

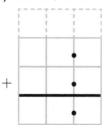

d) 63.4 + 12.6 + 1.5

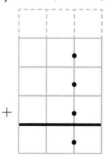

7. On a grid, line up the decimal points and add the numbers. You may need to regroup more than once.

a) 19.6 + 3.6   b) 37.9 + 30.5   c) 126.8 + 2.9   d) 314.5 + 56.7

8. Clara buys 3.8 kg of red apples and 2.9 kg of green apples. What is the total mass of the apples?

9. Jake weighs 45.9 kg and his dog, Spot, weighs 3.7 kg. What is their total weight in kg?

10. Subtract by crossing out ones and tenths blocks.

a) $2.8 - 0.6 =$ ___2.2___

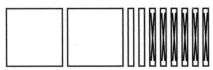

b) $3.5 - 1.4 =$ _____

c) $5.7 - 3.5 =$ _____

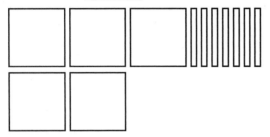

d) $8.9 - 4.3 =$ _____

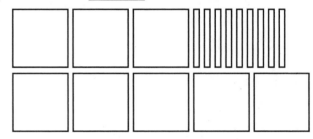

11. Represent some of the subtractions from Question 10 in tables by lining up the decimal points.

a) $2.8 - 0.6 =$ ___2.2___

	Ones	Tenths
	2	8
−	0	6
	2	2

b) $5.7 - 3.5 =$ _____

	Ones	Tenths
−		

c) $8.9 - 4.3 =$ _____

	Ones	Tenths
−		

12. Subtract the decimals by lining up the decimal points.

a) $10.7 - 10.3$

1	0	.	7
− 1	0	.	3
0	0	.	4

b) $20.5 - 10.2$

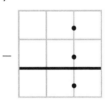

c) $13.4 - 2.2$

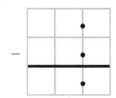

d) $16.4 - 0.3$

e) $52.5 - 11.5$

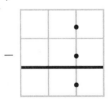

f) $63.7 - 2.6$

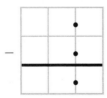

g) $78.8 - 7.1$

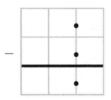

h) $95.1 - 93.0$

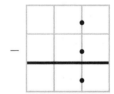

i) $4.8 - 4.4$

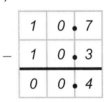

j) $21.5 - 1.4$

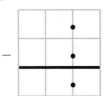

k) $45.5 - 12.4$

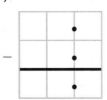

l) $79.8 - 42.7$

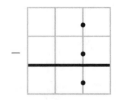

When subtracting decimals, you may have to regroup.

Example:

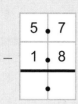

Regroup 1 one as 10 tenths.

13. Exchange 1 one for 10 tenths.

    a) 4 ones + 0 tenths = ___3___ ones + ___10___ tenths

    b) 8 ones + 0 tenths = _____ ones + _____ tenths

    c) 4 ones + 3 tenths = _____ ones + _____ tenths

    d) 6 ones + 8 tenths = _____ ones + _____ tenths

    e) 7 ones + 4 tenths = _____ ones + _____ tenths

    BONUS ▶ 9823 ones + 19 tenths = _____ ones + _____ tenths

14. Subtract the decimals. Put a decimal point in your answer on the grid.

    a) 8.1 − 5.8   b) 5.7 − 3.9   c) 6.1 − 4.2   d) 2.4 − 0.7

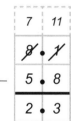 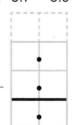 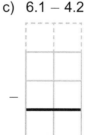 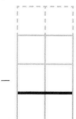

    e) 4.5 − 2.6   f) 31.1 − 22.2   g) 57.4 − 6.6   **BONUS ▶** 105.2 − 1.9

15. To calculate the sum, write the decimals as fractions with a common denominator.

    a) $0.27 + 0.6 = \dfrac{27}{100} + \dfrac{6}{10} = \dfrac{27}{100} + \dfrac{}{100} = \dfrac{}{100} =$ _____.____ ____

    b) $0.57 + 0.76 = \dfrac{57}{100} + \dfrac{76}{100} = \dfrac{}{100} =$ _____.____ ____

    c) $2.02 + 0.99 = \dfrac{}{100} + \dfrac{}{100} = \dfrac{}{100} =$ _____.____ ____

16. Subtract the decimals.

a) $8.7 - 2.6$

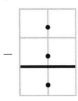

b) $29.4 - 13.1$

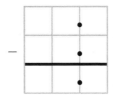

c) $75.8 - 43.6$

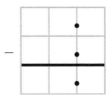

17. Add or subtract mentally.

a) $0.5 + 0.3 =$ _____

b) $4.9 - 2.8 =$ _____

c) $7.9 - 4.2 =$ _____

d) $2.3 + 1.2 =$ _____

e) $5.7 - 1.6 =$ _____

f) $6.7 - 2.5 =$ _____

g) $6.3 + 2.5 =$ _____

h) $4.3 - 2.1 =$ _____

i) $9.4 - 7.4 =$ _____

18. What is the difference in the thickness of the coins?

a) a quarter (1.6 mm) and a dime (1.2 mm)

_____

_____

b) a nickel (1.8 mm) and a quarter (1.6 mm)

_____

_____

19. Sara made fruit drink by mixing 1.2 L of juice with 0.9 L of ginger ale.
How many litres of fruit drink did she make?

_____

_____

_____

20. A large leopard, including its head, body, and tail, is 3.3 m long.
Its tail is 1.4 m long. What is the length of the leopard's head
and body altogether?

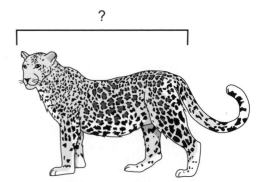

?

_____

_____

_____

1. Draw an arrow pointing to 0.0 or 1.0 to show whether the circled decimal is closer to 0.0 or 1.0.

   a)
   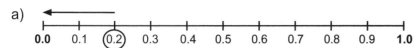

   b)
   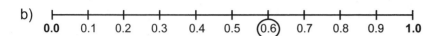

   c)
   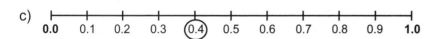

   d)
   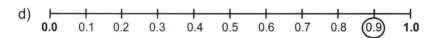

2. a) Which decimal numbers are closer to the number?

   i) 0.0 _____   ii) 1.0 _____

   b) Why is 0.5 a special case? _____

3. Draw an arrow to show which whole number you would round the circled number to.
   Then round the number.

   a)
   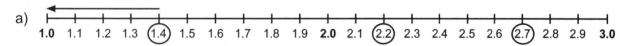

   Round to   _1.0_   _____   _____

   b)
   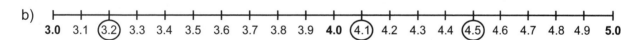

   Round to _____   _____   _____

   BONUS ▶
   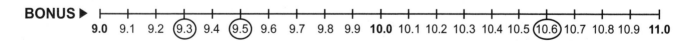

   Round to   _____ _____   _____

4. Circle the correct answer.

   a) 2.9 is closer to: 2.0 or 3.0   b) 1.4 is closer to: 1.0 or 2.0

   c) 3.6 is closer to: 3.0 or 4.0   d) 7.2 is closer to: 7.0 or 8.0

   e) 25.4 is closer to: 25.0 or 26.0   f) 48.8 is closer to: 48.0 or 49.0

   g) 93.6 is closer to: 93.0 or 94.0   h) 59.6 is closer to: 59.0 or 60.0

5. Estimate by rounding to the nearest *one*.

a) 6.8 ⟶ $\boxed{7}$ b) 12.7 $\boxed{}$ c) 34.8 $\boxed{}$ d) 9.5 $\boxed{}$

  $\underline{+\ 1.2}$ ⟶ + $\boxed{1}$ $\underline{+\ 5.4}$ + $\boxed{}$ $\underline{+\ 14.7}$ + $\boxed{}$ $\underline{-\ 6.3}$ − $\boxed{}$

  $\boxed{8}$ $\boxed{}$ $\boxed{}$ $\boxed{}$

e) 46.2 − 15.8   f) 31.9 − 19.5   g) 165.2 − 54.7   h) 149.7 − 24.9

  ≈ $\underline{46 - 16}$ ≈ _____   ≈ _____   ≈ _____

  = $\underline{30}$ = _____   = _____   = _____

i) 115.4 − 9.7   j) 78.6 + 10.9   k) 220.3 − 4.6   l) 27.5 + 31.7

  ≈ _____   ≈ _____   ≈ _____   ≈ _____

  = _____   = _____   = _____   = _____

6. Estimate by rounding to the nearest *one*.

a) Oscar the puppy is 39.6 cm long. His basket is 60.3 cm long.
    Approximately how much longer is the basket than Oscar?

    _____

    _____

b) The longest paddle in a shed is 154.6 cm long. The shortest paddle is 49.7 cm long.
    Approximately how much longer is the long paddle?

    _____

    _____

c) Emma's favourite hike is 16.7 km long. Her second favourite
    hike is 9.5 km long.

    i)   Approximately how much longer is her favourite hike?

    ii) Approximately how long are the hikes altogether?

d) The shallow end of a pool is 0.4 m deep, and the deep end is 4.5 m deep.

    i)   Approximately how much deeper is the deep end than the shallow end?

    ii) Does it make sense to use estimation for this problem? Explain.

NS4-58 Tenths and Hundredths (Fractions)

One dime is $\frac{1}{10}$ of a dollar. One cent is $\frac{1}{100}$ of a dollar.

1. Write the fraction of a dollar the amount represents.

   a) 4 cents ⬜   b) 3 dimes ⬜   c) 6 dimes ⬜   d) 34 cents ⬜

2. Write how many cents the dimes are worth. Then write a fraction equation.

   a) 3 dimes = __30__ cents

   $\frac{3}{10} = \frac{30}{100}$

   b) 7 dimes = _____ cents

   c) 8 dimes = _____ cents

   d) 5 dimes = _____ cents

3. Complete the table.

	Fraction of a Dollar (Tenths)	Number of Dimes	Number of Cents	Fraction of a Dollar (Hundredths)
a)	$\frac{4}{10}$	4	40	$\frac{40}{100}$
b)		6		
c)			90	
d)	$\frac{3}{10}$			

4. Yu says 37 pennies are worth more than 5 dimes because 37 coins are more than 5 coins. Is she right? Explain.

5. Shade the same amount in the second square. Then count by 10s to write the number of hundredths.

   a)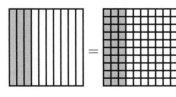

   $\frac{3}{10} = \frac{}{100}$

   b)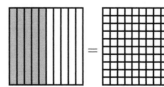

   $\frac{5}{10} = \frac{}{100}$

6. Count the columns to write the tenths. Count by 10s to write the hundredths.

a)

Picture	Tenths	Hundredths
	$\dfrac{2}{10}$	$\dfrac{20}{100}$

b)

Picture	Tenths	Hundredths
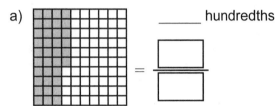		

7. Count the number of hundredths. Write your answer two ways.
Hint: Count by tens and then by ones.

a)   _____ hundredths

$= \dfrac{\boxed{}}{\boxed{}}$

b) 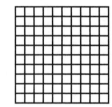 _____ hundredths

$= \dfrac{\boxed{}}{\boxed{}}$

8. Shade the fraction.

a) $\dfrac{47}{100}$

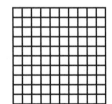

b) $\dfrac{3}{10}$

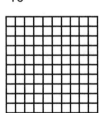

c) 5 hundredths

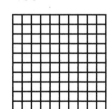

d) 4 tenths

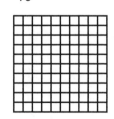

9. Shade the fraction. Then circle the greater fraction in the pair.

a) $\dfrac{38}{100}$ ⬜ $\dfrac{6}{10}$ ⬜

b) $\dfrac{4}{100}$ ⬜ $\dfrac{7}{10}$ ⬜

10. Marko says that $\dfrac{17}{100}$ is greater than $\dfrac{8}{10}$ because 17 is greater than 8.

Is Marko correct? Explain.

_____

_____

NS4-59 Decimal Hundredths

A **hundredth** (or $\frac{1}{100}$) can be represented in different ways.

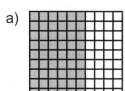 ← A hundredth of the distance from 0 to 1

Examples: $\frac{1}{100} = 0.01$, $\frac{8}{100} = 0.08$, $\frac{37}{100} = 0.37$

1. Write a fraction for the shaded part of the hundreds block. Then write the fraction as a decimal.
   Hint: Count by 10s for each column or row that is shaded.

a) $\frac{60}{100} = 0.60$

b)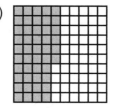

c)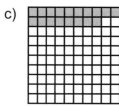

d)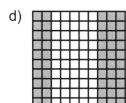

e)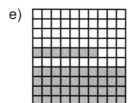

BONUS ▶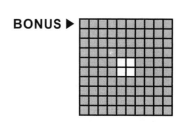

2. Write the decimal hundredths.

   a) 18 hundredths = _____   b) 9 hundredths = _____   c) 90 hundredths = _____

   d) 10 hundredths = _____   e) 52 hundredths = _____   f) 99 hundredths = _____

3. Shade the same amount in the second square. Then count by 10s to find the number
   of hundredths. Write your answer as a fraction and a decimal.

a)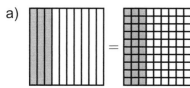

$\frac{3}{10} = \frac{30}{100}$

0.3 = _0.30_

b)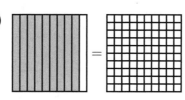

$\frac{9}{10} = \frac{}{100}$

0.9 = _____

c)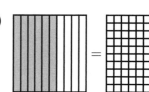

$\frac{6}{10} = \frac{}{100}$

0.6 = _____

4. a) Complete the table.

	Fraction Tenths	Fraction Hundredths	Picture	Decimal Tenths	Decimal Hundredths
i)	$\dfrac{2}{10}$	$\dfrac{20}{100}$	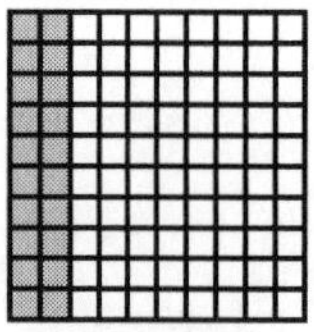	0.2	0.20
ii)					
iii)					

b) i) Circle the decimal that is greatest and underline the decimal that is least: 0.40   0.20   0.70

   ii) Use your answer to part b) i) to write the decimals from least to greatest:

   _____ < _____ < _____

c) Use your answer to part a) to write the decimals from least to greatest: 0.40   0.20   0.70

   _____ < _____ < _____

d) Are the answers in part b) ii) and part c) the same? _____

5. Complete the table.

	Fraction Tenths	Fraction Hundredths	Decimal Tenths	Decimal Hundredths
a)	$\dfrac{4}{10}$	$\dfrac{40}{100}$	0.4	0.40
b)	$\dfrac{3}{10}$			
c)			0.8	
d)				0.10

1. Describe the shaded parts in two ways.

a)
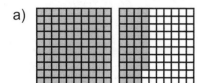

<u>   1.38   </u> = <u>   1   </u> one <u>   3   </u> tenths <u>   8   </u> hundredths

b)
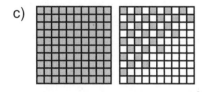

<u>   </u> = <u>   </u> ones <u>   </u> tenths <u>   </u> hundredths

c)
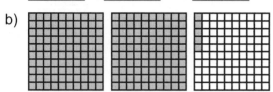

<u>   </u> = <u>   </u> one <u>   </u> tenths <u>   </u> hundredths

d)
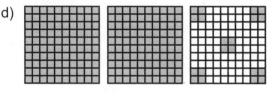

<u>   </u> = <u>   </u> ones <u>   </u> tenths <u>   </u> hundredths

2. Fill in the blanks.

a) 71 hundredths = <u> 7 </u> tenths <u> 1 </u> hundredth

$$\frac{71}{100} = 0.\underline{\ 7\ }\ \underline{\ 1\ }$$

b) 28 hundredths = <u>   </u> tenths <u>   </u> hundredths

$$\frac{}{100} = 0.\underline{\ \ \ }\ \underline{\ \ \ }$$

c) 41 hundredths = <u>   </u> tenths <u>   </u> hundredth

$$\frac{}{100} = 0.\underline{\ \ \ }\ \underline{\ \ \ }$$

d) 60 hundredths = <u>   </u> tenths <u>   </u> hundredths

$$\frac{}{100} = 0.\underline{\ \ \ }\ \underline{\ \ \ }$$

e) 53 hundredths = <u>   </u> tenths <u>   </u> hundredths

$$\frac{}{100} = 0.\underline{\ \ \ }\ \underline{\ \ \ }$$

f) 12 hundredths = <u>   </u> tenth <u>   </u> hundredths

$$\frac{}{100} = 0.\underline{\ \ \ }\ \underline{\ \ \ }$$

g) 36 hundredths = <u>   </u> tenths <u>   </u> hundredths

$$\frac{}{100} = 0.\underline{\ \ \ }\ \underline{\ \ \ }$$

h) 92 hundredths = <u>   </u> tenths <u>   </u> hundredths

$$\frac{}{100} = 0.\underline{\ \ \ }\ \underline{\ \ \ }$$

3. Describe the decimal in two ways.

a) $3.70 = \underline{\ 3\ }$ ones $\underline{\ 7\ }$ tenths $\underline{\ 0\ }$ hundredths b) $0.04 = \underline{\ 0\ }$ tenths $\underline{\ 4\ }$ hundredths

$\quad\quad = \underline{\ 3 \text{ and } 70 \text{ hundredths}\ }$ $\quad\quad\quad\quad\quad\quad = \underline{\ 4 \text{ hundredths}\ }$

c) $0.52 = \underline{\quad}$ tenths $\underline{\quad}$ hundredths d) $6.02 = \underline{\quad}$ ones $\underline{\quad}$ tenths $\underline{\quad}$ hundredths

$\quad\quad = \underline{\quad\quad\quad\quad\quad}$ $\quad\quad\quad\quad = \underline{\quad\quad\quad\quad\quad}$

e) $0.83 = \underline{\quad}$ tenths $\underline{\quad}$ hundredths f) $5.55 = \underline{\quad}$ ones $\underline{\quad}$ tenths $\underline{\quad}$ hundredths

$\quad\quad = \underline{\quad\quad\quad\quad\quad}$ $\quad\quad\quad\quad = \underline{\quad\quad\quad\quad\quad}$

g) $1.06 = \underline{\quad}$ one $\underline{\quad}$ tenths $\underline{\quad}$ hundredths h) $8.90 = \underline{\quad}$ ones $\underline{\quad}$ tenths $\underline{\quad}$ hundredths

$\quad\quad = \underline{\quad\quad\quad\quad\quad}$ $\quad\quad\quad\quad = \underline{\quad\quad\quad\quad\quad}$

4. Write the number in expanded form.

a) $2.95 = \underline{\quad\quad} + \underline{\quad\quad} + \underline{\quad\quad}$

b) $5408.41 = \underline{\quad\quad} + \underline{\quad\quad} + \underline{\quad\quad} + \underline{\quad\quad} + \underline{\quad\quad} + \underline{\quad\quad}$

c) $237.06 = \underline{\quad\quad} + \underline{\quad\quad} + \underline{\quad\quad} + \underline{\quad\quad} + \underline{\quad\quad}$

d) $67.23 = \underline{\quad\quad} + \underline{\quad\quad} + \underline{\quad\quad} + \underline{\quad\quad}$

Cameron describes the distance covered on a number line in two ways.

43 hundredths = 4 tenths 3 hundredths   0.43

0.00   0.10   0.20   0.30   0.40   0.50   0.60   0.70   0.80   0.90   1.00

---

5. Write the distance covered in two ways.

A   B   C   D

0.00   0.10   0.20   0.30   0.40   0.50   0.60   0.70   0.80   0.90   1.00

A. $\underline{\quad}$ tenth $\underline{\quad}$ hundredths   B. $\underline{\quad}$ tenths $\underline{\quad}$ hundredths

$= \underline{\quad}$ hundredths $\quad\quad\quad\quad = \underline{\quad}$ hundredths

C. $\underline{\quad}$ tenths $\underline{\quad}$ hundredths   D. $\underline{\quad}$ tenths $\underline{\quad}$ hundredths

$= \underline{\quad}$ hundredths $\quad\quad\quad\quad = \underline{\quad}$ hundredths

REMINDER ▶ A metre is 100 centimetres.

6. What part of a metre is the length shown? Write your answer as a decimal and a fraction.

a) 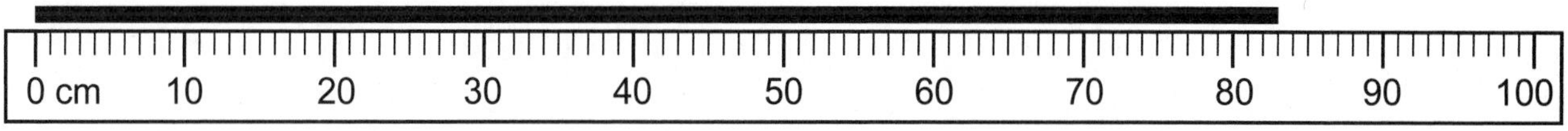

83 cm = *0.83* m = $\frac{83}{100}$ m

b) 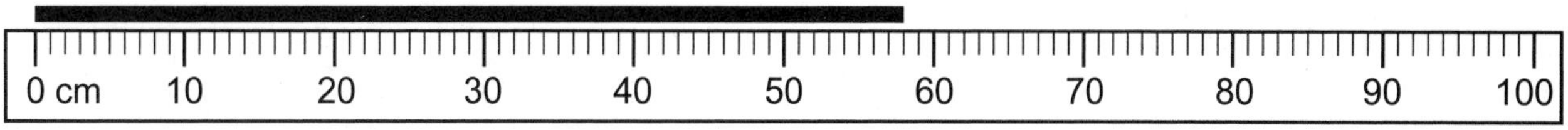

58 cm = ________ m = ☐ m

c) 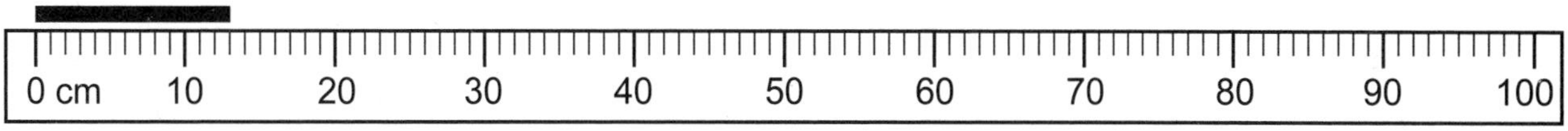

13 cm = ________ m = ☐ m

d) 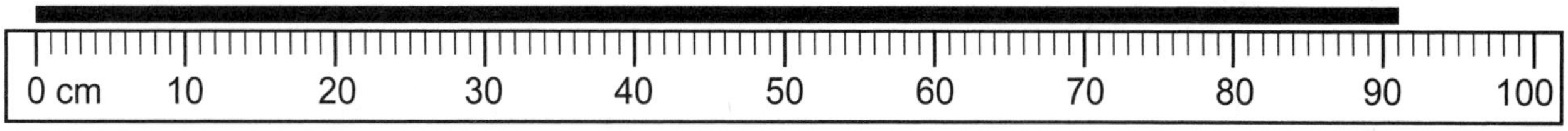

91 cm = ________ m = ☐ m

e) 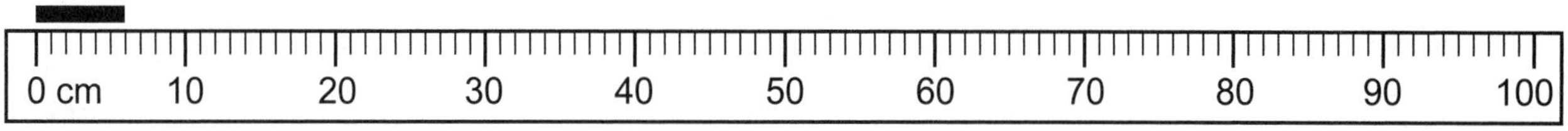

6 cm = ________ m = ☐ m

f) 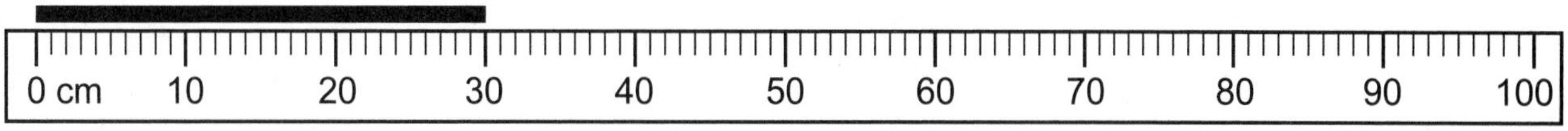

30 cm = ________ m = ☐ m

A base ten representation for decimal tenths and hundredths:

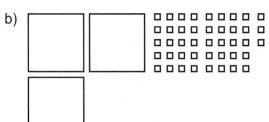

| 1 one | 1 tenth | 1 hundredth | 1 one = 10 tenths | 1 tenth = 10 hundredths |

1. Regroup so that each place value has a single digit.

a)

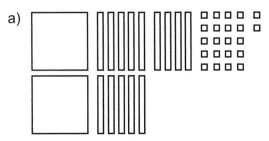

2 ones + 14 tenths + 22 hundredths

= *3 ones + 6 tenths + 2 hundredths*

b)

3 ones + 43 hundredths

= _____

c)

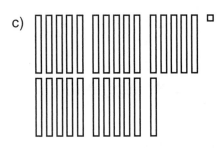

26 tenths + 1 hundredth

= _____

d)

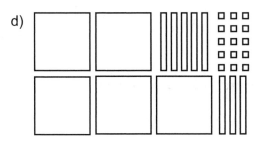

5 ones + 8 tenths + 15 hundredths

= _____

2. Regroup so that each place value has a single digit.

a) 5 ones + 12 tenths + 17 hundredths = ___6___ ones + ___3___ tenths + ___7___ hundredths

b) 16 tenths + 22 hundredths = _____ one + _____ tenths + _____ hundredths

c) 7 ones + 13 tenths + 20 hundredths = _____ ones + _____ tenths + _____ hundredths

d) 1 one + 76 tenths + 16 hundredths = _____ ones + _____ tenths + _____ hundredths

BONUS ▶ 9 ones + 13 tenths + 52 hundredths = _____ ten + _____ ones + _____ tenths
+ _____ hundredths

3. Add by lining up the decimal points. You may need to regroup more than once.

a) $7.15 + 2.46$

b) $34.64 + 21.27$

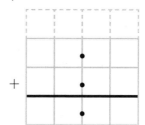

c) $68.89 + 22.31$

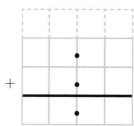

4. On a grid, line up the decimal points and then add.

a) $34.9 + 5.77$ b) $62.95 + 27.1$ c) $53.8 + 8.03$ d) $1.46 + 17.8$

e) $0.41 + 3.8$ f) $4.25 + 1.9$ g) $7.8 + 12.64$ h) $2.54 + 53.7$

5. Exchange 1 tenth for 10 hundredths.

a) 6 tenths + 0 hundredths = ___5___ tenths + ___10___ hundredths

b) 9 tenths + 4 hundredths = _____ tenths + _____ hundredths

c) 1 tenth + 6 hundredths = _____ tenths + _____ hundredths

d) 8 tenths + 8 hundredths = _____ tenths + _____ hundredths

6. Subtract by lining up the decimal points. You may need to regroup more than once.

a) $1.75 - 0.68$

b) $4.12 - 0.09$

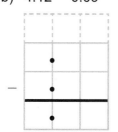

c) $7.23 - 6.14$

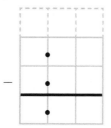

d) $9.14 - 1.06$

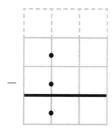

e) $43.52 - 25.9$

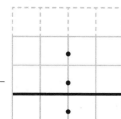

f) $35.3 - 18.49$

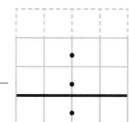

g) $63.07 - 2.7$

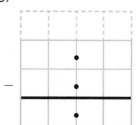

h) $78.4 - 54.72$

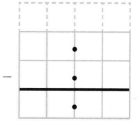

7. a) Iva draws three lines. The first line is 14.4 cm long, the second line is 25.62 cm long, and the third line is 6.08 cm long. What is the total length of the lines?

b) Iva erases 2.4 cm from the line that is 6.08 cm long. What is the total length of the lines now?

c) Did you need to know which line she erased from to answer the question in part b)? Explain.

The tables show how to represent money in cent notation and in dollar notation.

	Cent Notation	Dollar (Decimal) Notation
Sixty-five cents	65¢	$0.65 *dimes* *cents*

	Cent Notation	Dollar (Decimal) Notation
Seven cents	7¢	$0.07 *dimes* *cents*

The dot between the 0 and the number of dimes is called a **decimal point**.

1. Write the total amount of money in cent notation and in dollar (decimal) notation.

a)

Dimes	Cents
3	4

= __34__ ¢ = $__0.34__

b)

Dimes	Cents
0	5

= _____¢ = $_____

c)

Dimes	Cents
4	3

= _____¢ = $_____

d)

Dimes	Cents
8	7

= _____¢ = $_____

e)

Dimes	Cents
5	4

= _____¢ = $_____

f)

Dimes	Cents
0	9

= _____¢ = $_____

g)

Dimes	Cents
0	2

= _____¢ = $_____

h)

Dimes	Cents
7	5

= _____¢ = $_____

i)

Dimes	Cents
0	1

= _____¢ = $_____

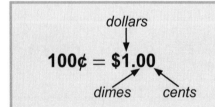

100¢ = **$1.00**

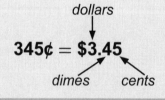

345¢ = **$3.45**

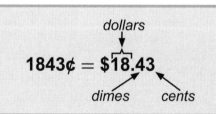

1843¢ = **$18.43**

2. Complete the table.

	Amount in ¢	Dollars	Dimes	Cents	Amount in $
a)	143¢	1	4	3	$1.43
b)	47¢				
c)	325¢				
d)	3¢				
e)	2816¢				

3. Write the amount in cent notation.

a) $3.00 = _____ b) $0.60 = _____ c) $0.09 = _____ d) $1.00 = _____

e) $7.00 = _____ f) $12.00 = _____ g) $15.00 = _____ h) $1.99 = _____

i) $1.51 = _____ j) $0.98 = _____ k) $0.03 = _____ l) $0.08 = _____

4. Write the amount in dollar notation.

a) 254¢ = _$2.54_ b) 103¢ = _____ c) 216¢ = _____ d) 375¢ = _____

e) 300¢ = _____ f) 4¢ = _____ g) 7¢ = _____ h) 90¢ = _____

i) 600¢ = _____ j) 99¢ = _____ k) 1200¢ = _____ l) 1604¢ = _____

5. Complete the table as shown in part a).

	Dollars		Cents		Total
a)		= _$3_		= _35¢_	_$3.35_
b)		= _____		= _____	
c)		= _____		= _____	_____
d)		= _____		= _____	_____

6. Lela paid for a pencil with 3 coins. The pencil cost $0.75. Which coins did she use?

7. Ansel bought a pack of markers for $3.50. He paid for it with 5 coins. Draw the money he used.

8. Show two ways to make $5.25 with 6 coins.

NS4-63 Money Math

1. You have $10. Find the difference owed when you need to pay the given amount.

	Amount to Pay	Paid	Calculation	Difference Owed
a)	$2	$10	$10 − $2	$8
b)	$4	$10		
c)	$7	$10		
d)	$3	$10		
e)	$6	$10		

2. You have $1. Find the difference owed when you need to pay the given amount.

	Amount to Pay	Paid	Calculation	Difference Owed
a)	70¢	$1	100¢ − 70¢	30¢
b)	40¢	$1		
c)	60¢	$1		
d)	90¢	$1		
e)	50¢	$1		
f)	10¢	$1		

3. Find the difference to the next highest dollar.

a) $12.30 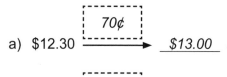 $13.00

b) $15.20  $16.00

c) $14.40  _____

d) $11.70  _____

e) $21.60 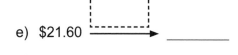 _____

f) $35.10 _____

g) $59.40 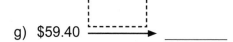 _____

BONUS ▶ $87.80 _____

You need to pay $16.40. You pay with a 20-dollar bill ($20.00). What is the difference owed?

Step 1: Find the next highest whole dollar after $16. $17

Step 2: Write the amount of money given. $20

Step 3: Find the differences in the steps.   60¢, $3

Step 4: Add the differences. $3.60

Difference owed = $3.60

4. You need to pay the given amount. You have a 20-dollar bill. Find the difference owed.

a)

Difference owed

= _____

b)

Difference owed

= _____

c)

Difference owed

= _____

BONUS ▶ You need to pay the given amount. You have a 50-dollar bill.
Find the difference owed.

d)

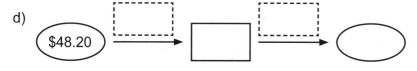

Difference owed

= _____

e)

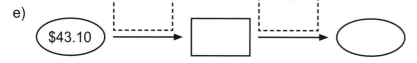

Difference owed

= _____

f)

Difference owed

= _____

g)

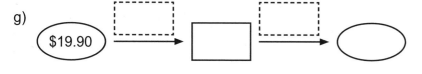

Difference owed

= _____

h)

Difference owed

= _____

5. You need to pay the given amount. You have a 20-dollar bill. Find the difference owed.

a)

$13.25 → | 5¢ | → $13.30 → | 70¢ | → $14 → | $6 | → $20

Difference owed

= $6.75

b)

$17.65 → [ ] → [ ] → [ ] → $20

Difference owed

=

c)

$12.15 → [ ] → [ ] → [ ] → ( )

Difference owed

=

6. Round the given amount to the nearest nickel by rounding the number of cents to the nearest multiple of 5.

	Money	$	¢	Cents Rounded to the Nearest Nickel	Money Rounded to the Nearest Nickel
a)	$18.43	$18	43¢	45¢	$18.45
b)	$22.21				
c)	$49.78				
d)	$13.07				
e)	$59.97				

7. You need to pay the amount shown. You have a 50-dollar bill. Round the amount to the nearest nickel. Then find the difference owed.

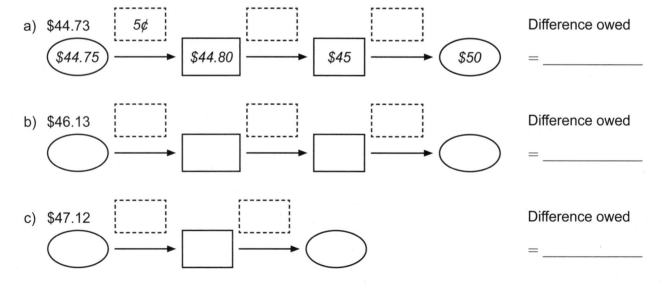

a) $44.73 | 5¢ | [ ] [ ]

$44.75 → $44.80 → $45 → $50

Difference owed

=

b) $46.13 [ ] [ ] [ ]

( ) → [ ] → [ ] → ( )

Difference owed

=

c) $47.12 [ ] [ ]

( ) → [ ] → ( )

Difference owed

=

1. Some apples are inside a box and some are outside. Draw the missing apples in the box.

   a)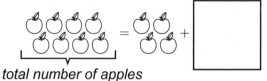

   total number of apples

   b)

   c)

   total number of apples

   d)

2. Draw the missing apples in the box. Then write the missing number in the smaller box.

   a)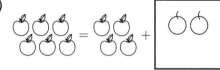

   6   =   4   +   2

   b)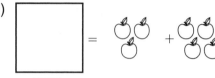

   ☐   =   3   +   4

   c)

   3   +   5   =   ☐

   d)

   9   =   ☐   +   4

Finding the missing number in an equation is called **solving** the equation.

---

3. Draw a picture for the equation. Use your picture to solve the equation.

   a) $5 + \boxed{} = 9$

   b) $\boxed{} + 4 = 10$

4. Solve the equation by guessing and checking.

   a) $\boxed{} + 4 = 21$

   b) $3 + \boxed{} = 30$

   c) $47 = 12 + \boxed{}$

   d) $73 = \boxed{} + 8$

5. Some apples are inside a box and some are outside. Draw the missing apples in the box.

a)  − ☐ = ☐

b) ☐ − ☐ = ☐

c) ☐ = ☐ − ☐

d) ☐ = ☐ − ☐

6. Draw the missing apples in the box. Then write the missing number in the smaller box.

a) ☐ − ☐ = ☐

    5 − 2 = ☐

b) ☐ − ☐ = ☐

    ☐ − 3 = 6

c) ☐ = ☐ − ☐

    6 = 8 − ☐

d) ☐ = ☐ − ☐

    7 = ☐ − 3

7. Draw a picture for the equation. Use your picture to solve the equation.

a) $10 - \boxed{} = 7$

b) $5 = \boxed{} - 3$

8. Solve the equation by guessing and checking.

a) $\boxed{} - 21 = 7$

b) $40 - \boxed{} = 15$

c) $89 = \boxed{} - 1$

BONUS ▶ $\boxed{} = 94 - 63$

1. Draw the same number of apples in each box. Write the equation for the picture.

a)

□ + □ = 10

_____

b)

[ ] + [ ] + [ ] = (apples)

_____

2. Draw a picture for the equation. Use your picture to solve the equation.

a)
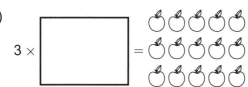

3 × [4] = 12

b)
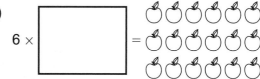

2 × □ = 12

c)

3 × [ ] = 15

d)

6 × [ ] = 18

e)

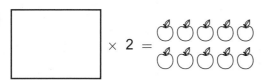

□ × 2 = 10

f)

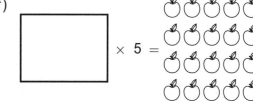

□ × 5 = 20

3. How many apples should be in the box? Write the number.

a) $2 \times \boxed{3} = $ 🍎🍎🍎 🍎🍎🍎

b) $2 \times \boxed{} = $ 🍎🍎 🍎🍎

c) $3 \times $ 🍎🍎 🍎🍎 $= \boxed{}$

d) $\boxed{} \times 4 = $ 🍎🍎🍎🍎 🍎🍎🍎🍎

e) $\boxed{} \times 3 = $ 🍎🍎🍎 🍎🍎🍎 🍎🍎🍎

f) $3 \times $ 🍎🍎 🍎🍎 🍎🍎 $= \boxed{}$

g) $\boxed{} \times 2 = $ 🍎🍎🍎🍎 🍎🍎🍎🍎

h) $7 \times $ 🍎🍎 🍎🍎 $= \boxed{}$

BONUS ▶ There are 10 apples in the bag. What number goes in the box?

$3 \times$ 🛍️ 🍎🍎 $= \boxed{}$

4. Solve the equation by guessing and checking.

a) $5 \times \boxed{} = 30$

b) $18 \div 2 = \boxed{}$

c) $30 \div \boxed{} = 5$

d) $\boxed{} \times 7 = 77$

e) $24 \div \boxed{} = 6$

f) $\boxed{} \div 5 = 10$

g) $5 \times 40 = \boxed{}$

h) $\boxed{} \div 4 = 7$

5. Rewrite the multiplication as division, then solve the equation.

a) $\boxed{} \times 2 = 26$

b) $96 = 3 \times \boxed{}$

c) $\boxed{} \times 4 = 80$

d) $100 = \boxed{} \times 20$

e) $\boxed{} \times 4 = 88$

f) $150 = 50 \times \boxed{}$

PA4-14 Totals and Equations

1. Circle the equations where the unknown is by itself.

$$x = 7 + 2 \qquad w + 5 = 10 \qquad 5 - 3 = a \qquad 6 - b = 4 \qquad k = 12 \div 3$$

Total	
Part 1	Part 2

There are 3 equations for a total and two parts:

Total = Part 1 + Part 2
Part 1 = Total − Part 2
Part 2 = Total − Part 1

2. Write three equations for the table. Circle the equation where the unknown is by itself.

a)

k	
8	5

$$\underset{\text{Total}}{k} = \underset{\text{Part 1}}{8} + \underset{\text{Part 2}}{5}$$

$$\underset{\text{Part 1}}{8} = \underset{\text{Total}}{k} - \underset{\text{Part 2}}{5}$$

$$\underset{\text{Part 2}}{5} = \underset{\text{Total}}{k} - \underset{\text{Part 1}}{8}$$

b)

24	
21	k

$$\underset{\text{Total}}{\rule{1cm}{0.4pt}} = \underset{\text{Part 1}}{\rule{1cm}{0.4pt}} + \underset{\text{Part 2}}{\rule{1cm}{0.4pt}}$$

$$\underset{\text{Part 1}}{\rule{1cm}{0.4pt}} = \underset{\text{Total}}{\rule{1cm}{0.4pt}} - \underset{\text{Part 2}}{\rule{1cm}{0.4pt}}$$

$$\underset{\text{Part 2}}{\rule{1cm}{0.4pt}} = \underset{\text{Total}}{\rule{1cm}{0.4pt}} - \underset{\text{Part 1}}{\rule{1cm}{0.4pt}}$$

c)

17	
k	3

$$\underset{\text{Total}}{\rule{1cm}{0.4pt}} = \rule{1cm}{0.4pt} + \rule{1cm}{0.4pt}$$

$$\underset{\text{Part 1}}{\rule{1cm}{0.4pt}} = \rule{1cm}{0.4pt} - \rule{1cm}{0.4pt}$$

$$\underset{\text{Part 2}}{\rule{1cm}{0.4pt}} = \rule{1cm}{0.4pt} - \rule{1cm}{0.4pt}$$

d)

k	
215	65

$$\underset{\text{Total}}{\rule{1cm}{0.4pt}} = \rule{1cm}{0.4pt} + \rule{1cm}{0.4pt}$$

$$\underset{\text{Part 1}}{\rule{1cm}{0.4pt}} = \rule{1cm}{0.4pt} - \rule{1cm}{0.4pt}$$

$$\underset{\text{Part 2}}{\rule{1cm}{0.4pt}} = \rule{1cm}{0.4pt} - \rule{1cm}{0.4pt}$$

e)

97	
k	18

$$\underset{\text{Total}}{\rule{1cm}{0.4pt}} = \rule{1cm}{0.4pt} + \rule{1cm}{0.4pt}$$

$$\underset{\text{Part 1}}{\rule{1cm}{0.4pt}} = \rule{1cm}{0.4pt} - \rule{1cm}{0.4pt}$$

$$\underset{\text{Part 2}}{\rule{1cm}{0.4pt}} = \rule{1cm}{0.4pt} - \rule{1cm}{0.4pt}$$

f)

312	
78	k

$$\underset{\text{Total}}{\rule{1cm}{0.4pt}} = \rule{1cm}{0.4pt} + \rule{1cm}{0.4pt}$$

$$\underset{\text{Part 1}}{\rule{1cm}{0.4pt}} = \rule{1cm}{0.4pt} - \rule{1cm}{0.4pt}$$

$$\underset{\text{Part 2}}{\rule{1cm}{0.4pt}} = \rule{1cm}{0.4pt} - \rule{1cm}{0.4pt}$$

3. Write an equation where m is by itself.

a)

17	
12	m

$m = 17 - 12$

b)

8	
m	5

_____

c)

m	
11	2

_____

d)

9	
m	3

_____

4. Fill in the table. Write m for the number you are not given.

		Green Grapes	Purple Grapes	Total Number of Grapes	Equation
a)	6 green grapes 14 grapes in total	6	m	14	$m = 14 - 6$
b)	5 green grapes 3 purple grapes				
c)	11 grapes in total 9 green grapes				
d)	7 purple grapes 16 grapes altogether				
e)	34 purple grapes 21 green grapes				
f)	71 grapes altogether 45 purple grapes				

BONUS ▶

	Green Grapes	Purple Grapes	Total Number of Grapes	Equation
131 purple grapes 26 green grapes				

5. Circle the total in the story. Then write an equation and solve it.

a) 6 green grapes
⟨9 grapes altogether⟩
x purple grapes

$x = 9 - 6$
$x = 3$

b) 3 green grapes
4 purple grapes
x grapes altogether

c) 11 grapes altogether
7 purple grapes
x green grapes

d) There are 6 cats.
There are 12 dogs.
There are x pets altogether.

e) There are 9 marbles.
x of them are red.
5 of them are not red.

f) Rick has 8 cousins.
x of them are boys.
3 of them are girls.

Larger Part	
Smaller Part	Difference

There are three equations for a difference and two parts:

Difference = Larger Part − Smaller Part

Larger Part = Smaller Part + Difference

Smaller Part = Larger Part − Difference

1. Write three equations for the table. Circle the equation where the unknown is by itself.

a)

10	
4	b

$$\underline{\hspace{2cm}} = \underline{\hspace{2cm}} - \underline{\hspace{2cm}}$$
Difference   Larger Part   Smaller Part

$$\underline{\hspace{2cm}} = \underline{\hspace{2cm}} + \underline{\hspace{2cm}}$$
Larger Part   Smaller Part   Difference

$$\underline{\hspace{2cm}} = \underline{\hspace{2cm}} - \underline{\hspace{2cm}}$$
Smaller Part   Larger Part   Difference

b)

b	
4	10

$$\underline{\hspace{2cm}} = \underline{\hspace{1cm}} - \underline{\hspace{1cm}}$$
Difference

$$\underline{\hspace{2cm}} = \underline{\hspace{1cm}} + \underline{\hspace{1cm}}$$
Larger Part

$$\underline{\hspace{2cm}} = \underline{\hspace{1cm}} - \underline{\hspace{1cm}}$$
Smaller Part

c)

34	
b	9

$$\underline{\hspace{2cm}} = \underline{\hspace{1cm}} - \underline{\hspace{1cm}}$$
Difference

$$\underline{\hspace{2cm}} = \underline{\hspace{1cm}} + \underline{\hspace{1cm}}$$
Larger Part

$$\underline{\hspace{2cm}} = \underline{\hspace{1cm}} - \underline{\hspace{1cm}}$$
Smaller Part

2. Fill in the table. Write x for the number you are not given. Circle the part that is larger.
Write an equation where the unknown is by itself.

		Parts		Difference	Equation
		Cats	Dogs		
a)	7 cats; 12 more dogs than cats	7	(x)	12	x = 12 + 7
b)	5 cats; 3 dogs				
c)	11 more dogs than cats; 8 cats				
d)	9 dogs; 3 fewer cats than dogs				
e)	17 dogs; 13 fewer dogs than cats				

BONUS ▶

100 cats; 20 fewer dogs than cats					

3. Circle the part that is larger. Underline the difference.

a) There are (9 hats.)
   There are *x* scarves.
   There are 4 more hats
   than scarves.

b) There are *x* hats.
   There are 7 scarves.
   There are 5 fewer hats
   than scarves.

c) There are 5 hats.
   There are 6 scarves.
   There are *x* fewer hats
   than scarves.

4. Fill in the table. Write *x* for the number you are not given. Circle the part that is larger.

	Problem	What Is Compared?	How Many?	Difference	Equation and Solution
a)	Jun has 48 American stamps in his collection. He has 12 more American stamps than Canadian stamps. How many Canadian stamps does he have?	American stamps	(48)		$x = 48 - 12$
		Canadian stamps	*x*	12	$x = 36$
b)	Lela has 12 red marbles. She has 8 green marbles. How many more red marbles than green marbles does she have?				
c)	There are 13 dogs in a shelter. There are 7 more cats than dogs in the shelter. How many cats are there?				
d)	A bulldog weighs 7 kg less than a boxer. The boxer weighs 35 kg. How much does the bulldog weigh?				

5. Write an equation where the unknown is by itself. Then solve the equation.

a) Dory hikes 8 km on Saturday. She hikes 3 km more on Sunday than on Saturday. How many kilometres did she hike on Sunday?

b) 17 cars are parked in the school parking lot. There are 8 fewer vans than cars in the same lot. How many vans are there?

c) A dalmatian weighs 29 kg. A dingo weighs 8 kg less. How much does the dingo weigh?

d) Aputik biked 42 km on Saturday. On Sunday, she biked 12 km more than on Saturday. How far did she bike on Sunday?

e) Carl counted 38 robins in his backyard on Monday and 29 robins on Tuesday. How many more robins flew through Carl's backyard on Monday?

f) Sally counted 72 shooting stars on one night. The next night she saw 24 fewer stars than on the first night. How many shooting stars did she see on the second night?

PA4-16 Addition and Subtraction Word Problems

1. Fill in the table. Write x for the number you need to find. Cross out the information you do not use.

	Problem	Parts	How Many?	Difference / Total	Equation and Solution
a)	Neka has 4 kg of apples and 5 kg of pears. How many kilograms of fruit does he have?	apples	4 kg	Difference: ~~____~~	$x = 4 + 5$
		pears	5 kg	Total: __x__	$x = 9$
b)	Karen biked 47 km on Monday. She biked 54 km on Tuesday. How far did Karen bike in two days?	distance on Monday		Difference: ____	
				Total: ____	
c)	Alice raised $32 for charity. Ben raised $9 less than Alice. How much money did Ben raise?			Difference: ____	
				Total: ____	
d)	Alexa bought 3000 millilitres of apple juice. She bought 2000 more millilitres of apple juice than plum juice. How much plum juice did she buy?			Difference: ____	
				Total: ____	
e)	The cafeteria sold 350 cartons of milk. 198 of them were cartons of white milk. The rest were chocolate milk. How many cartons of chocolate milk did the cafeteria sell?			Difference: ____	
				Total: ____	
f)	The height of Mount Kilimanjaro is 5895 m. That is 2953 m less than the height of Mount Everest. How tall is Mount Everest?			Difference: ____	
				Total: ____	

2. The world's tallest tree is about 116 m tall. The Horseshoe Falls at Niagara Falls is about 51 m tall. How much taller is the tallest tree than the Horseshoe Falls?

3. Solve the problem. Use your answer from part i) as data for part ii).

a) i) Tom bought 9 hockey cards and 6 baseball cards. How many cards did he buy altogether?

ii) Tom gave away 5 cards. How many does he have left?

b) There are 24 players on a hockey team, and 15 of them are new to the team.

i) How many players are not new to the team?

ii) How many more new players than not new players are on the team?

4. Solve the two-step problem.

a) Sara bought 8 red jelly beans and 5 white jelly beans. She ate 4 of them. How many jelly beans does she have left?

b) Marko downloaded 7 songs. He downloaded 3 more songs than movies. How many songs and movies did he download altogether?

c) Ray had $32. He bought the book, magazine, and scissors below. How much money does he have left?

$7.00

$6.00

$9.00

5. Ivan invited 10 friends from school and 8 friends from camp to his birthday party.

a) How many more friends from school than friends from camp were supposed to be at the party?

b) Two friends from school and three friends from camp could not come to the party. How many friends were at the party?

c) Were there more friends from school or more friends from camp at the party? How many more?

6. The table shows the number of cars arriving at the train station parking lot. No cars leave the lot in the morning.

a) How many cars are parked in the lot at 7:00 a.m.?

b) How many cars are parked in the lot at 8:00 a.m.?

c) There are 1008 spaces in total in the lot. How many are still available at 8:00 a.m.?

Before 6:00 a.m.	378
From 6:00 a.m. to 7:00 a.m.	459
From 7:00 a.m. to 8:00 a.m.	125

PA4-17 Models and Times as Many

1. Draw a model for the story.

   a) Don has 5 stamps. Jasmin has 3 times as many as Don does.

   Don's stamps: | 5 |

   Jasmin's stamps: | 5 | 5 | 5 |

   b) There are 3 red grapes. There are 5 times as many green grapes as red grapes.

   _____

   _____

   c) There are 16 green pears. There are 4 times as many red pears as green pears.

   _____

   _____

   d) Anne has 4 markers. Fred has 5 times as many markers as Anne.

   _____

   _____

2. Solve the problem by drawing a model.

   a) Ansel has 6 stamps. Jen has 3 times as many stamps as Ansel. How many stamps do they have altogether?

   Ansel's stamps: | 6 | 6 stamps

   Jen's stamps: | 6 | 6 | 6 | 18 stamps

   6 + 18 = 24, so Jen and Ansel have 24 stamps altogether.

   b) Lewis studies spiders and scorpions. He has 6 spiders and twice as many scorpions. How many spiders and scorpions does he have altogether?

   _____

   _____

   _____

   c) There are 4 hamsters in a store. There are six times as many mice in the store. How many mice and hamsters are there altogether?

3. Draw a model for the story.

a) Mandy has four times as many stickers as Ethan.

Mandy's stickers: ⬚⬚⬚⬚

Ethan's stickers: ⬚

b) Mary is three times as old as Armand.

_____

_____

c) There are five times as many green grapes as red grapes.

_____

_____

d) A book is two times thicker than a notebook.

_____

_____

e) There are three times as many lizards as snakes in the zoo.

_____

_____

4. Draw a model for the story. Then write the given number beside the correct bar.

a) There are 20 carrots. There are 4 times as many carrots as potatoes.

carrots: 20 ⬚⬚⬚⬚

potatoes: ⬚

b) There are 30 cars in a parking lot. There are 6 times as many cars as vans in the lot.

_____

_____

c) Nora chopped up 70 carrots and twice as many little tomatoes for a salad.

_____

_____

5. Draw the model.

a) Jayden needs three times as many blueberries as raspberries to make jam.
He needs 6 cups more blueberries than raspberries. He needs 12 cups of
berries altogether.

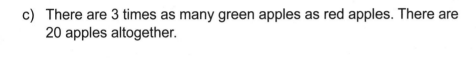

blueberries:

raspberries:

b) Billy's building is 5 times as tall as Grace's. Billy's building is 20 floors taller
than Grace's.

_____

_____

c) There are 3 times as many green apples as red apples. There are
20 apples altogether.

_____

_____

d) There are twice as many apricots as peaches. There are 32 more apricots
than peaches.

_____

_____

6. All the blocks are the same size. What is the size of each block?

a)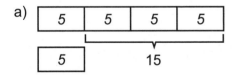

b)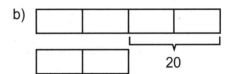

c)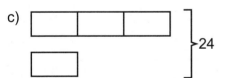

d)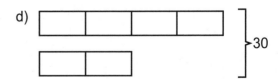

e)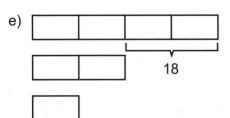

f)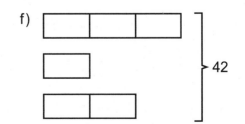

7. Draw the model. Find the size of one block in the model. Then solve the problem.

a) Zack has four times as many stickers as Alex. Zack has 15 more stickers than Alex. How many stickers does each person have?

Zack's stickers:

| 5 | 5 | 5 | 5 |

Alex's stickers:

| 5 | 15

Zack has __20__ stickers and Alex has __5__ stickers.

b) Hanna is three times as old as Marcel. Hanna is 8 years older than Marcel. How old are Hanna and Marcel?

_____

_____

Hanna is _____ years old and Marcel is _____ years old.

c) There are five times as many green apples as red apples. There are 24 apples altogether. How many apples of each colour are there?

_____

_____

There are _____ green apples and _____ red apples.

d) A granola recipe calls for seven times as much oatmeal as nuts. Avril wants to make 400 grams of granola. How many grams of nuts and oatmeal does she need?

_____

_____

Avril needs _____ grams of oatmeal and _____ grams of nuts.

e) A rottweiler weighs five times as much as a Scottish terrier. The Scottish terrier weighs 36 kg less than the rottweiler. How much does each dog weigh?

_____

_____

The Scottish terrier weighs _____ kg and the rottweiler weighs _____ kg.

f) A pair of pants costs twice as much as a shirt. Fred paid $42 for a pair of pants and a shirt. How much did each item cost?

BONUS ▶ How much would Fred pay for two pairs of pants and three shirts?

When the larger part is 3 times the size of the smaller part, we say the **scale factor** is 3.

Smaller Part [ ]

Larger Part [ ][ ][ ]

You can find one part from another part using the scale factor.

Larger Part = Smaller Part × Scale Factor

Smaller Part = Larger Part ÷ Scale Factor

1. Circle the larger part and underline the smaller part in the problem. Then fill in the blanks for the equation where the unknown is by itself and cross out the other equation.

   a) There are 21 cats and w dogs. There are three times as many (dogs) as cats.

   | w | = | 21 | × | 3 | or | ~~~~~~~~~~~~~~ | ~~=~~ | ~~~~~~~~~~~~~~ | ~~÷~~ | ~~~~~~~~~~~~~~ |
   | Larger Part | | Smaller Part | | Scale Factor | | ~~Smaller Part~~ | | ~~Larger Part~~ | | ~~Scale Factor~~ |

   b) There are 6 plums and w pears. There are 2 times as many plums as pears.

   | _____ | = | _____ | × | _____ | or | _____ | = | _____ | ÷ | _____ |
   | Larger Part | | Smaller Part | | Scale Factor | | Smaller Part | | Larger Part | | Scale Factor |

   c) There are 8 cats and w dogs. There are 4 times as many dogs as cats.

   | _____ | = | _____ | × | _____ | or | _____ | = | _____ | ÷ | _____ |
   | Larger Part | | Smaller Part | | Scale Factor | | Smaller Part | | Larger Part | | Scale Factor |

   d) There are 12 adults in a chess club. There are twice as many teenagers as adults in the chess club.

   | _____ | = | _____ | × | _____ | or | _____ | = | _____ | ÷ | _____ |
   | Larger Part | | Smaller Part | | Scale Factor | | Smaller Part | | Larger Part | | Scale Factor |

2. Fill in the table. Write w for the number you are not given.
   Hint: Circle the larger part and underline the smaller part.

	Problem	Part	How Many?	Equation
a)	There are 20 green apples in a box. There are 4 times as many (green apples) as red apples.	green apples	20	$20 \div 4 = w$
		red apples	w	
b)	There are 16 pears. There are twice as many pears as bananas.			
c)	There are 6 cats in a shelter. There are three times as many dogs as cats in the shelter.			
d)	Sun planted 40 bean seeds. That is 5 times as many as the corn seeds she planted. How many corn seeds did she plant?			

3. Complete the table.

	Total Number of Things	Number of Sets	Number in Each Set	Multiplication or Division Equation
a)	w	6	3	6 × 3 = w
b)	20	4	w	20 ÷ 4 = w
c)	18	w	6	
d)	24	2	w	
e)	w	4	7	
f)	35	w	5	

4. Fill in the table. Write w to show what you don't know. Then write a multiplication or division equation in the last column and solve the problem.

		Total Number of Things	Number of Sets	Number in Each Set	Multiplication or Division Equation
a)	36 people 3 vans	36	3	w	36 ÷ 3 = w __12__ people in each van
b)	10 marbles in each jar 6 jars				_____ _____ marbles
c)	35 flowers 5 pots				_____ _____ flowers in each pot
d)	6 chairs at each table 7 tables				_____ _____ chairs

5. a) A soccer league has 8 teams with 11 players each. How many players are in the league?

b) A birch tree is 15 m tall. A maple tree is twice as tall the birch. How tall is the maple tree?

c) Zara is 35 years old. Zara is 5 times as old as Ken. How old is Ken?

d) A box of pencils costs $2. How much do 25 boxes of pencils cost?

e) Ella paid $15 for three scarves. If all the scarves cost the same amount, how much did each one cost?

BONUS ▶ A male mountain gorilla weighs 200 kg, four times as much as a male chimpanzee. How much does the chimpanzee weigh?

ME4-9 Perimeter

The distance around the outside of a shape is the perimeter of the shape.

The edges of the squares in this figure measure 1 cm.

The perimeter of the figure is 6 cm.

1. Each edge is 1 cm long. Trace the perimeter of the figure. Find the perimeter in centimetres.

   a)   b)   c)

   _____ cm   _____ cm   _____ cm

2. Each edge is 5 mm long. Count by 5s to find the perimeter in millimetres.

   a)   b)   c)   d)

   _____ mm   _____ mm   _____ mm   _____ mm

3. Draw your own figure on the centimetre grid and find its perimeter. (Do not use diagonal lines.)

4. What unit would you use to measure the perimeter: cm, m, or km?

   a) a book: _____   b) a forest: _____   c) a basketball court: _____

   d) a classroom: _____   e) a province: _____   f) a basketball hoop: _____

5. Why might you want to use millimetres to measure a perimeter?

_____

_____

_____

6. Add to find the perimeter of the figure.

a)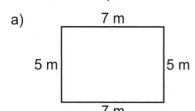

Perimeter = _____

b)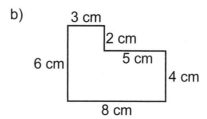

Perimeter = _____

c)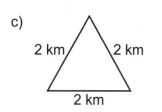

Perimeter = _____

d)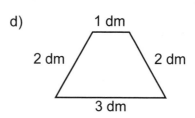

Perimeter = _____

7. Measure the perimeter of the figure in millimetres. Use a ruler.

a)

b)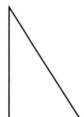

c)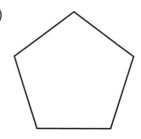

_____   _____   _____

8. Estimate the perimeter of the figure in centimetres. Then measure the actual perimeter with a ruler.

a)

Estimated perimeter = _____

Actual perimeter = _____

b)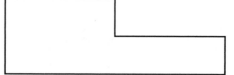

Estimated perimeter = _____

Actual perimeter = _____

ME4-10 Calculating Perimeter

1. The pictures show the designs for two gardens. Find the perimeter of each garden by writing an addition equation.

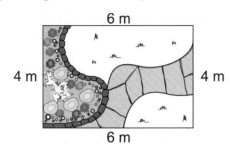

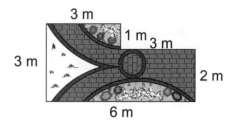

_____   _____

2. Write the number of boxes along the width and the length of the rectangle. Then write an addition equation and find the perimeter (in centimetres).

a)

Length = _____ cm

Width = _____ cm

Perimeter = _____

b)

Length = _____ cm

Width = _____ cm

Perimeter = _____

c)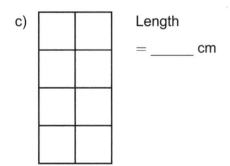

Length = _____ cm

Width = _____ cm

Perimeter = _____

d)

Width = _____ cm

Length = _____ cm

Perimeter = _____

3. Write a rule for finding the perimeter of a rectangle from its length (ℓ) and width (w).

_____

A rectangle has perimeter 12 m. Each side is an exact number of metres long.

What are the dimensions of the rectangle? Let's try different widths. Try 1 m first.

The widths add to 2 m.
The missing lengths are 12 m − 2 m = 10 m altogether.
Each length is 10 m ÷ 2 = 5 m.

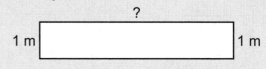

4. a) The widths add to _____ m.

b) The missing lengths are 12 m − _____ m = _____ m altogether.

c) Each length is _____ m ÷ 2 = _____ m.

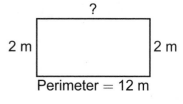

Perimeter = 12 m

5. a) The widths add to _____ m.

b) The missing lengths are _____ altogether.

c) Each length is _____ m.

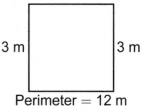

Perimeter = 12 m

6. Find the missing sides. (The pictures are not drawn to scale.)

a) Perimeter = 14 m

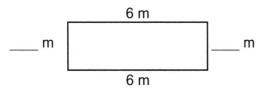

b) Perimeter = 14 cm

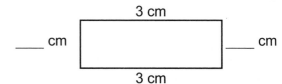

c) Perimeter = 10 m

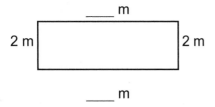

d) Perimeter = 14 cm

7. Find all rectangles with the given perimeter (with lengths and widths that are exact numbers of units).

Perimeter = 6 units	
Width	**Length**

Perimeter = 10 units	
Width	**Length**

Perimeter = 16 units	
Width	**Length**

Perimeter = 18 units	
Width	**Length**

8. Write a rule for finding the perimeter of a square from its side length.

ME4-11 Reflections

1. Draw the line of symmetry.

a)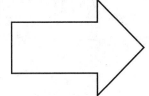

b)

c)

2. The dashed line is the mirror line. Draw the mirror image.

a)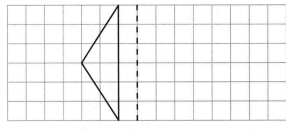

b)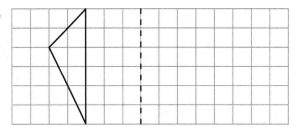

c)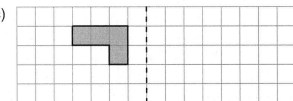

d)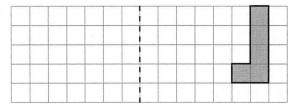

3. The dashed line is the reflecting line. Draw the mirror image.

a)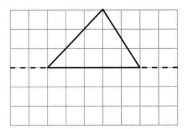

b)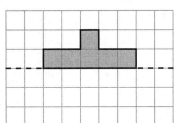

c)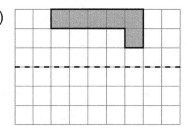

d)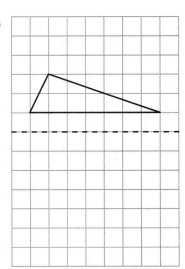

e)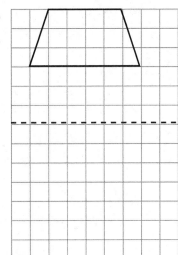

BONUS ▶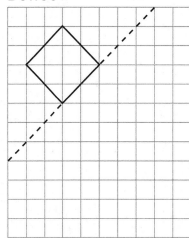

4. Draw the reflections of the shape and points in the line.

a)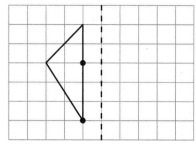

b)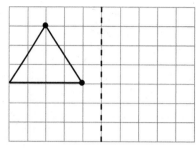

c)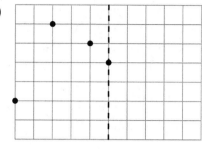

d)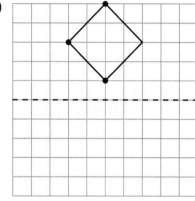

e)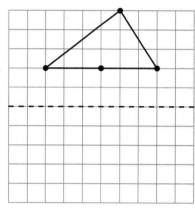

f)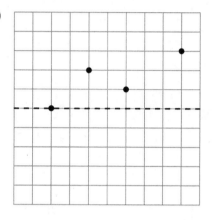

5. Draw the reflection of the shape by first finding the reflections of its vertices.

a)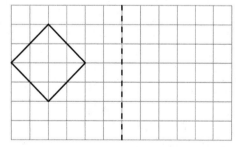

b)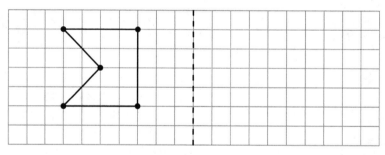

c)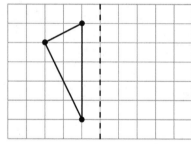

d)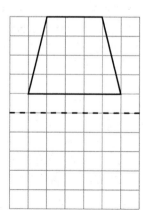

e)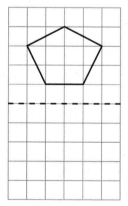

6. a) Extend the pattern by reflecting the shape in vertical lines.

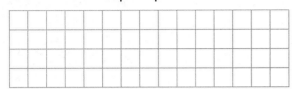

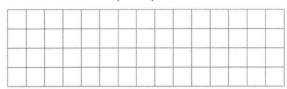

b) Draw the 12ᵗʰ shape in pattern A.

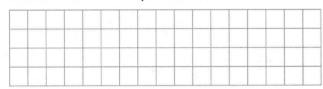

c) Draw the 57ᵗʰ shape in pattern A.

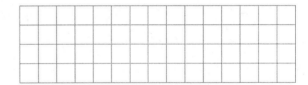

7. David made a pattern by alternating between reflecting and translating a shape.

a) Continue the pattern.

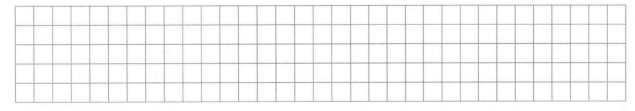

b) Draw the core of the pattern.

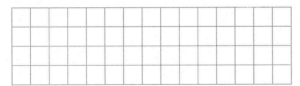

c) Draw the 15ᵗʰ shape in the pattern.

d) Draw the 24ᵗʰ shape in the pattern.

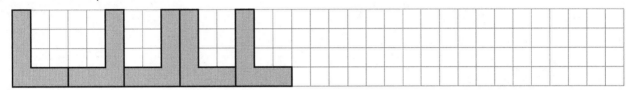

8. a) Use reflections to draw your own pattern of shapes.

b) Draw the core of your pattern.

ME4-12 Identifying Reflections

1. Find the vertical line of reflection.

a) 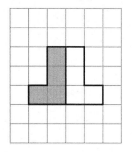   b) 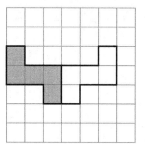   c) 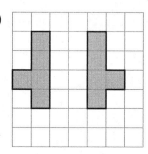   d)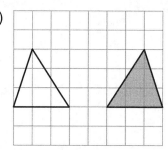

2. Find the horizontal line of reflection.

a) 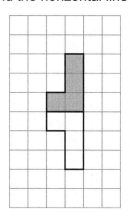   b) 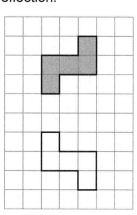   c) 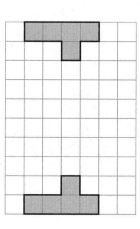   d)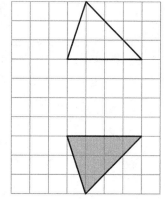

3. Connect the corresponding vertices to find the line of reflection.

a) 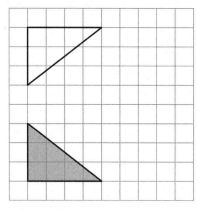   b) 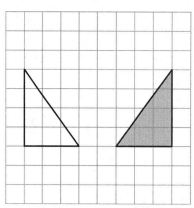   c)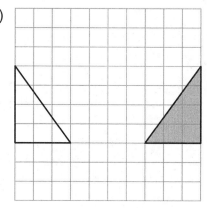

d) 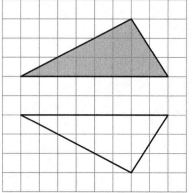   e) 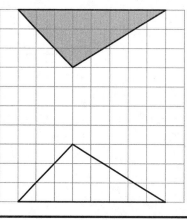   BONUS ▶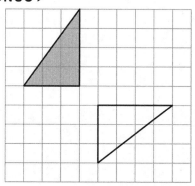

Measurement 4-12

4. Circle the pairs that can be created by a reflection.

a)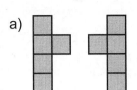

b)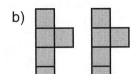

c)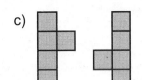

d)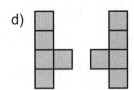

e)

f)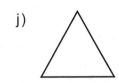

g)

h)

i)

j)

BONUS ▶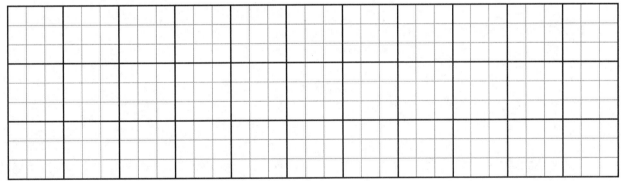

BONUS ▶ Use a ruler to draw the lines of reflection in the circled pairs in Question 4.

5. a) Colour the squares in the first 3 by 3 tile using at least two colours. Create a pattern by reflecting your tile vertically and horizontally.

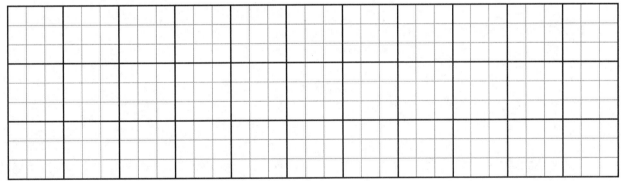

b) What would the 6ᵗʰ tile in the third column look like?

c) What would the 7ᵗʰ tile in the fourth column look like?

The **area** of a flat shape is the amount of space it takes up.

A **square centimetre** (cm²) is a unit for measuring area.

A square with sides 1 cm has an area of 1 cm².

1. Find the area of the figure in square centimetres.

a)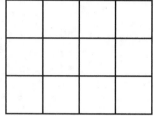

Area = _____ cm²

b)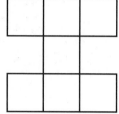

Area = _____ cm²

c)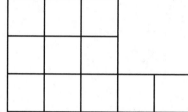

Area = _____ cm²

2. Using a ruler, draw lines to join the marks and divide the rectangle into square centimetres.

a)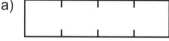

Area = _____ cm²

b)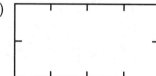

Area = _____ cm²

c)

Area = _____ cm²

3. Find the area of the rectangles in square centimetres.

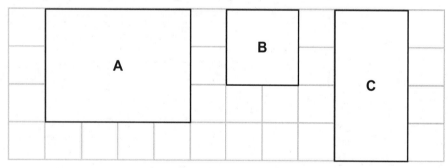

Area of A = _____ cm²   Area of B = _____ cm²   Area of C = _____ cm²

4. Use 1 cm grid paper.

   a) Draw two different rectangles with an area of 8 cm².

   b) Draw two figures that are not rectangles with an area of 8 cm².

   c) Draw several shapes and find their area.

   d) Draw three different rectangles with an area of 12 cm².

ME4-14 Area in Square Metres

> A **square metre** (m^2) is a unit for measuring area.
>
> A square with sides 1 m has an area of 1 m^2.
>
>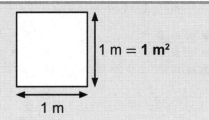
>
> 1 m = **1 m^2**
>
> 1 m
>
> Four unfolded pages from a newspaper are about 1 m^2.

1. Shelly measured the areas of objects at school, but she forgot to write down the units.
    Fill in the blank with "m^2" or "cm^2."

    a) The wall measures 8 _____.

    b) The book cover measures 375 _____.

    c) The sticky note measures 15 _____.

    d) The parking lot measures 475 _____.

2. Choose a unit of measure for the area. Estimate and then measure the area of the object.

	Object	Unit	Estimate	Actual Area
a)	blackboard			
b)	JUMP Math AP Book			
c)	hallway			
d)	desk			
e)	light switch			

3. Ethan says that since there are 100 cm in 1 m, there must be 100 cm^2 in 1 m^2.
    Is he correct? Explain.

    _____

    _____

    _____

BONUS ▶ Why might someone measure a large area in cm^2?

    _____

    _____

    _____

ME4-15 Area of Rectangles

1. Write a multiplication statement for the array.

   a)

   b)

   c)

   d)

   _____   _____   _____   _____

2. Draw a dot in each box. Then write a multiplication statement that tells you
   the number of boxes in the rectangle.

   a)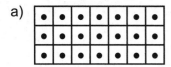

   b)

   c)

   d)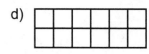

   _3 × 7 = 21____   _____   _____   _____

3. Write the number of boxes along the length and the width of the rectangle.
   Then write a multiplication equation for the area of the rectangle (in square units).

   a) 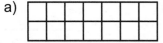 Width

   = ____

   Length = ____

   b) 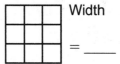 Width

   = ____

   Length = ____

   c) 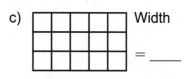 Width

   = ____

   Length = ____

   _____   _____   _____

4. Using a ruler, draw lines to join the marks and divide the rectangle into square centimetres.
   Write a multiplication equation for the area of the rectangle in square centimetres.

   a)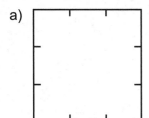

   b)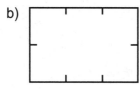

   c)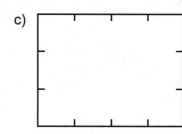

   Area = _____   Area = _____   Area = _____

5. How can you find the area of a rectangle from its length and width?

   _____

   _____

6. Measure the length and width of the rectangle. Find the area. Include the units!

a)

_____

b)

_____

c)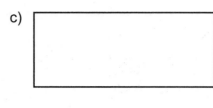

_____

7. Area is also measured in other square units. Predict the name of the unit.

a)

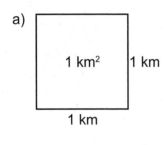

1 km²   1 km

1 km

___square kilometre___

b)

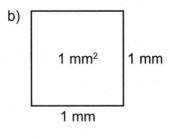

1 mm²   1 mm

1 mm

_____

c)

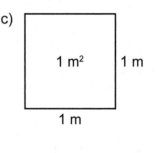

1 m²   1 m

1 m

_____

8. a) Calculate the area of each rectangle (include the units).

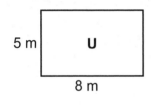

5 m   **U**

8 m

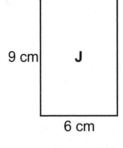

9 cm   **J**

6 cm

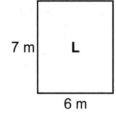

7 m   **L**

6 m

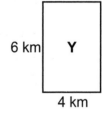

6 km   **Y**

4 km

Area = _____   Area = _____   Area = _____   Area = _____

b) List the rectangles from least area to greatest area: _____ , _____ , _____ , _____

What does it spell? _____

9. Find the area of the rectangle using the length and the width. Include the units!

a) Length = 7 m   Width = 5 m

Area = ___35 m²___

b) Length = 9 m   Width = 2 m

Area = _____

c) Length = 8 cm   Width = 6 cm

Area = _____

d) Length = 7 cm

Width = 11 cm

Area = _____

e) Length = 9 m

Width = 12 m

Area = _____

f) Length = 12 cm

Width = 3 cm

Area = _____

ME4-16 More Area

1. a) Calculate the area of each figure. Each square represents 1 square centimetre.

i) **A.** **B.** **C.**

ii) **A.** 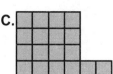 **B.** 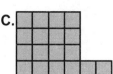 **C.**

Area of A = _____

Area of B = _____

Area of C = _____

Area of A = _____

Area of B = _____

Area of C = _____

iii) **A.** **C.** **B.**

iv) **A.** **C.** **B.**

Area of A = _____

Area of B = _____

Area of C = _____

Area of A = _____

Area of B = _____

Area of C = _____

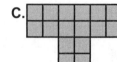

b) Draw a line to show how shape C can be divided into rectangles A and B in part a).

c) How can you get the area of shape C from the areas of rectangles A and B? Write an equation.

Area of C = _____

2. Draw a line to divide the figure into two rectangles. Use the areas of the rectangles to find the total area of the figure.

a)
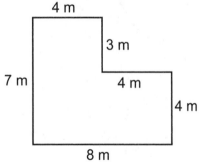
4 m
3 m
7 m
4 m
4 m
8 m

b)
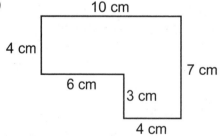
10 cm
4 cm
7 cm
6 cm
3 cm
4 cm

c)
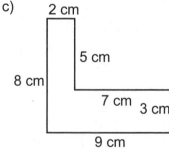
2 cm
5 cm
8 cm
7 cm 3 cm
9 cm

Area of rectangle 1 = _____

Area of rectangle 2 = _____

Total area = _____

Area of rectangle 1 = _____

Area of rectangle 2 = _____

Total area = _____

Area of rectangle 1 = _____

Area of rectangle 2 = _____

Total area = _____

3. a) A building is 8 storeys high. The wing is 5 storeys high. How many storeys high is the tower?

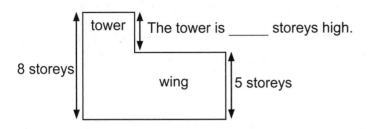

The tower is _____ storeys high.

b) The tower of a building is 10 m wide. The base is 50 m wide. How wide is the wing?

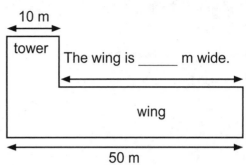

The wing is _____ m wide.

4. Find the missing side lengths. Divide the figure into two rectangles and find their areas. Then find the total area of the figure.

a)

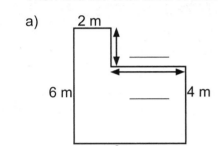

Area of rectangle 1 = _____

Area of rectangle 2 = _____

Total area = _____

b)

Area of rectangle 1 = _____

Area of rectangle 2 = _____

Total area = _____

5. Find the length of the rectangle.

a) Width = 2 cm   Perimeter = 12 cm

Length = _____

b) Width = 4 cm   Perimeter = 14 cm

Length = _____

6. Find the area of the rectangle using the clues.
Hint: First find the length of the rectangle.

a) Width = 2 cm   Perimeter = 10 cm

Area = _____

b) Width = 4 cm   Perimeter = 18 cm

Area = _____

7. On grid paper, draw a **square** with the given perimeter. Then find the area of the square.

a) Perimeter = 12 cm   Area = _____

b) Perimeter = 20 cm   Area = _____

ME4-17 Problems with Area and Perimeter

Area of rectangle = length × width

1. Find the area of the rectangle.

   a) Width = 3 m   Length = 6 m   b) Width = 2 m   Length = 9 m   c) Width = 6 cm   Length = 8 cm

   Area = _____ × _____   Area = _____ × _____   Area = _____ × _____

   = _____   = _____   = _____

2. Write an equation for the area of the rectangle. Then find the unknown length.

   a) Length = ℓ m   b) Length = ℓ m   c) Length = ℓ cm
      Width = 5 m   Width = 2 m   Width = 6 cm
      Area = 15 m²   Area = 12 m²   Area = 24 cm²

      $\ell \times 5 = 15$ _____   _____

      $\ell = 15 \div 5$ _____   _____

      $= 3$ _____   _____

3. Write an equation for the area of the rectangle. Then find the unknown width.

   a) Length = 5 m   b) Length = 7 m   c) Length = 10 cm
      Width = w m   Width = w m   Width = w cm
      Area = 20 m²   Area = 21 m²   Area = 40 cm²

      $5 \times w = 20$ _____   _____

      $w = 20 \div 5$ _____   _____

      $= 4$ _____   _____

4. a) A rectangle has an area of 24 m² and a width of 3 m. What is its length?

   b) A rectangle has an area of 10 cm² and a length of 5 cm. What is its width?

   c) A square has an area of 9 cm². What is its width?

5. A rectangle with length 3 cm and width 4 cm has area 12 cm².

   a) Find a different pair of numbers that multiply to equal 12.

   b) Draw a rectangle with length and width equal to your numbers.

$$3 \times 4 = 12$$

length   width   area

6. a) Measure the length and the width of each rectangle in centimetres. Find
the perimeter and area of each rectangle. Write the answers in the table.

```
A        5 cm            B           C               D


3 cm



E                               F
```

Shape	Perimeter	Area
A	3 cm + 5 cm + 3 cm + 5 cm = 16 cm	5 cm × 3 cm = 15 cm²
B		
C		
D		
E		
F		

b) Shape E has a greater perimeter than shape A. Does it also have a greater area? _____

c) Name two rectangles that have the same perimeter and different areas. _____ and _____

d) Write the shapes in order from greatest perimeter to least perimeter. _____

e) Write the shapes in order from greatest area to least area. _____

f) Are the orders in parts d) and e) the same? _____

g) Describe the difference between perimeter and area.

7. Will you use area or perimeter to find ...

a) the amount of paper needed to cover a bulletin board? _____

b) the distance around a field? _____

c) the amount of carpet needed for a room? _____

d) the amount of ribbon needed to make a border for a picture? _____

ME4-18 Problems and Puzzles

1. On grid paper, draw a rectangle with …

    a) an area of 10 square units and a perimeter of 14 units.

    b) an area of 12 square units and a perimeter of 14 units.

2. a) Find the area of the shaded word.

    b) There are 33 squares in the grid.
       How can you use your answer to part a)
       to find the number of unshaded squares?

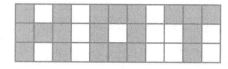

3. Raj wants to build a rectangular flowerbed of width 2 m and perimeter 12 m.

    a) Sketch the flowerbed on the grid.

    b) What is the length of the flowerbed?

    c) Raj wants to build a fence around the flowerbed.
       Fencing costs $3 per metre. How much will the fencing cost?

    d) Raj will plant 6 sunflower seeds on each square metre
       of land. Each sunflower seed costs 2¢. How much will the
       flowers cost altogether?

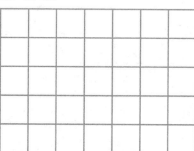

Note: The side of each square
in the grid represents 1 metre.

4. a) Draw two rectangles to show that figures with the same area
       can have different perimeters.

    b) Draw two rectangles to show that figures with the same perimeter
       can have different areas.

5. The area of your thumbnail is about 1 square centimetre (1 cm²).
Estimate the area of this rectangle using your thumbnail.
Then measure the sides of the rectangle and find its actual area.

6. On grid paper, draw a figure made of four squares.
Each square must share at least one edge with another square.

    a) How many different figures can you create?

    b) What is the area of the figures?

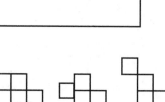

allowed   not allowed

    c) Which figure has the smallest perimeter?

    d) Ella thinks that two figures with the same perimeter and the same area
       have to be exactly the same shape and size. Is she correct? Explain.

ME4-19 Scale Drawings

1. Measure to find the actual dimensions of the room according to the scale.
   Then find the perimeter and area.

   a) Scale: 1 cm : 2 m

   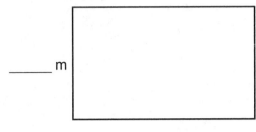

   _____ m

   _____ m

   Perimeter = _____

   Area = _____

   b) Scale: 1 cm : 3 m

   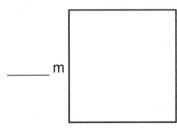

   _____ m

   _____ m

   Perimeter = _____

   Area = _____

2. a) The map shows the eastern-, western-, northern-, and southern-most capitals of
   Canada and Ottawa. Measure to find how far you would travel if you took the trip
   shown on the map. Scale: 1 cm : 300 km

   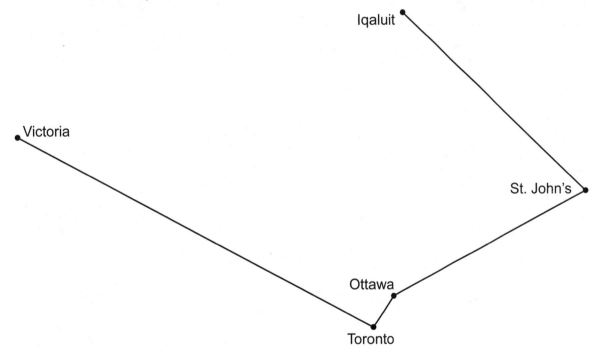

   Total distance: _____

   b) About how far is Victoria from Iqaluit?

3. This is a scale drawing of a park.

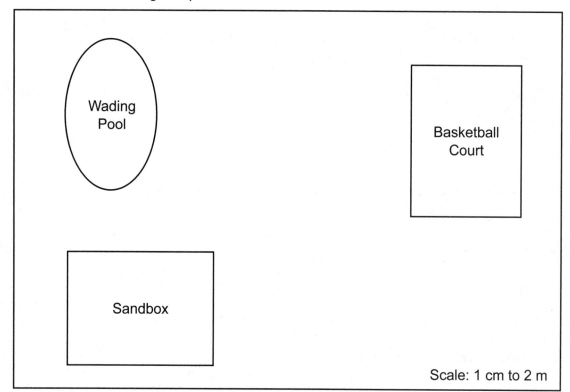

Wading Pool

Basketball Court

Sandbox

Scale: 1 cm to 2 m

a) What is the length and the width of the park in metres?

b) What is the perimeter and the area of the park in metres?

c) About how far is the basketball court from the wading pool?

d) What is the area of the basketball court in metres?

e) A swing set requires a 6 m by 4 m rectangular area. Add a scale drawing of the swing set to the park.

ME4-20 Grids and Maps

Use the grid to answer Questions 1–3.

	A	B	C	D	E
1	h	e	b	d	r
2	o	t	u	a	y
3	w	n	i	m	s

1. Find the hidden message by writing the letter that appears at the grid location.

   _____ _____ _____ _____ _____ _____ _____ _____   _____ _____ _____ _____
   B2   E1   B1   D2   E3   C2   E1   B1   A1   C2   B3   B2

2. Create a code for the word by writing the location of the letters in the grid.

   a) STAR: _E3_ _B2_ _D2_ _E1_

   b) HAT: _____ _____ _____

   c) OTTAWA: _____ _____ _____ _____ _____ _____

   d) WINDSOR: _____ _____ _____ _____ _____ _____ _____

   e) WHITEHORSE: _____ _____ _____ _____ _____ _____ _____ _____ _____ _____

3. Choose a word that you can write using the letters in the grid and write a code for it.

4. Draw the symbol in the grid. Write its location.

   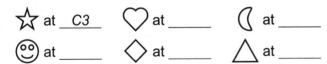 at _C3_   ♡ at _____   ☾ at _____

   😊 at _____   ◇ at _____   △ at _____

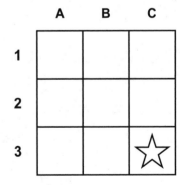

BONUS ▶ In a tic-tac-toe game, X took squares B2, C1, and A3.
O took squares A1, A2, and B1. Who won the game?

Use the map to answer Questions 5–7.

Scale: 1 cm to 100 m

(S) school   (L) library   (R) restaurant   (T) theatre

(H) hospital   (C) city hall   (P) picnic area   (M) mall

5. Find the landmark on the map and write its location.

   a) library: _____   b) city hall: _____

   c) theatre: _____   d) mall: _____

6. Where is the street on the map? Fill in the blanks.

   a) Main St. runs from __A3__ to __F3__   b) 4th Ave. runs from _____ to _____

   c) Green Ave. runs from _____ to _____   d) Park Rd. runs from _____ to _____

7. About how far apart are the two restaurants?

   BONUS ▶ Rani walks from the restaurant in C3 to the park entrance in E1.
   Draw her route on the map. About how far does she walk?

Digital clocks show hours and minutes separated by a colon.
This clock shows that 25 minutes have passed since 3 o'clock.
We say the time is 3:25 or 25 past (or after) 3.

hours minutes

We read 3:05 as "3 oh 5" or "5 past 3."

We read 3:00 as "3 o'clock."

1. Write the time in words and numbers.

a) ⏰ 08:17

_8:17_

17 past 8

b) ⏰ 03:42

_____

_____

c) ⏰ 12:05

_____

_____

d) ⏰ 14:23

_____

_____

e) ⏰ 9:00

_____

_____

f) ⏰ 23:11

_____

_____

g) ⏰ 7:59

_____

_____

h) ⏰ 16:16

_____

_____

i) ⏰ 12:30

_____

_____

2. Write the time the way it looks on a digital clock.

a) 7 past 5

☐☐ : ☐☐

b) 25 after 4

☐☐ : ☐☐

c) 51 minutes past 11

☐☐ : ☐☐

d) 10 past 5

☐☐ : ☐☐

e) 20 after 11

☐☐ : ☐☐

f) 50 minutes after 7

☐☐ : ☐☐

3. Write 20 past 2 in two ways.

☐☐ : ☐☐   ☐☐ : ☐☐

When the number of minutes after the hour is more than 30, we can tell the time by saying how many minutes until the hour changes.

Remember, there are 60 minutes in 1 hour.

Example: 60 − 45 = 15, so this clock shows 45 minutes after 10 or 15 minutes to 11.

4. How many minutes until the hour changes?

a) 11:50 is _____ minutes to 12.

b) 1:40 is _____ minutes to 2.

c) 3:35 is _____ minutes to 4.

d) 5:56 is _____ minutes to 6.

5. Write the time in minutes to the next hour.

a)

15 minutes to 9

b)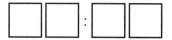

_____

c)

_____

d)

_____

e)

_____

f)

_____

6. Write the time the way it looks on a digital clock.

a) 7 minutes to 5

☐☐ : ☐☐

b) 25 minutes to 4

☐☐ : ☐☐

c) 10 minutes to 11

☐☐ : ☐☐

d) 2 minutes to 6

☐☐ : ☐☐

e) 20 minutes after 1

☐☐ : ☐☐

f) 5 minutes to 1

☐☐ : ☐☐

7. Write the time in two ways.

a)

_____

_____

b)

_____

_____

BONUS ▶

_____

_____

ME4-22 a.m., p.m., and the 24-Hour Clock

Use **a.m.** to show times from 12:00 midnight to 11:59.

Use **p.m.** to show times from 12:00 noon to 11:59.

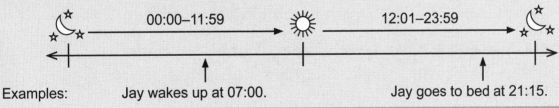

Examples: Jay wakes up at 7:00 a.m.   Jay goes to bed at 9:15 p.m.

1. Write "a.m." or "p.m."

   a) Lily eats breakfast at 7:30 _____   b) Ray goes to school at 8:15 _____

   c) School ends at 3:35 _____   d) Dinner is at 5:30 _____

   e) Karate class starts at 5:45 _____   f) The math test starts at 9:15 _____

   g) I stayed up until 1 _____   h) I slept in until 10 _____

On a 24-hour clock, the hours from 00:00 to 11:59 are before noon (a.m.), and 12:00 to 23:59 are after noon (p.m.).

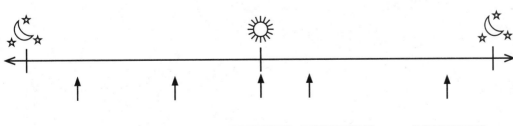

Examples: Jay wakes up at 07:00.   Jay goes to bed at 21:15.

2. Write "a.m." for times before noon and "p.m." for times after noon.

   a) 07:15 _____   b) 14:35 _____   c) 00:30 _____   d) 17:00 _____

   e) 12:15 _____   f) 21:17 _____   g) 10:40 _____   h) 23:58 _____

3. Fill in the times on the timeline.

   7:30 a.m.   noon   10:15 p.m.   14:25   4:25 a.m.

_____   _____   _____ _____   _____

4. Fill in the table.

a)
a.m.	1:00	2:00	3:00	4:00	5:00	6:00	7:00	8:00	9:00	10:00	11:00	12:00
24 hour	01:00											

b)
p.m.	1:00	2:00	3:00	4:00	5:00	6:00	7:00	8:00	9:00	10:00	11:00	12:00
24 hour	13:00											

5. Write the time the way it would look on a 24-hour clock.

a) 7:00 a.m.   b) 7:00 p.m.   c) 9:30 a.m.   d) 9:30 p.m.

   _____07:00_____   _____   _____   _____

e) 6:15 a.m.   f) 3:45 p.m.   g) 2:20 p.m.   h) 11:54 a.m.

   _____   _____   _____   _____

i) 4:23 p.m.   j) 1:17 p.m.   k) 8:48 a.m.   l) 11:19 p.m.

   _____   _____   _____   _____

6. The time is from a 24-hour clock. Write it the way you would for a 12-hour clock.

a) 14:00   b) 02:00   c) 08:30   d) 20:30

   ___2:00 p.m.___   _____   _____   _____

e) 07:45   f) 19:45   g) 22:20   h) 11:38

   _____   _____   _____   _____

i) 10:15   j) 23:45   k) 16:20   **BONUS ▶** 00:15

   _____   _____   _____   _____

7. Name an activity you usually do in the a.m. and an activity that you usually do in the p.m.

8 o'clock

It is 8 o'clock.
The hour hand is on the 8.
The minute hand is on the 12.

The time is 8:00.

1. Write the time two ways.

a)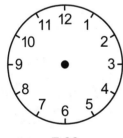

_____6 o'clock_____

_____ : _____

b)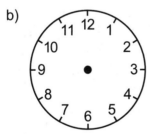

_____

_____ : _____

c)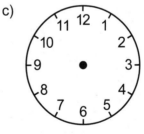

_____

_____ : _____

d)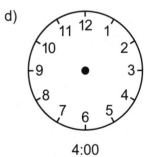

_____

_____ : _____

2. Write the time in numbers.

a) 7 o'clock   b) 5 o'clock   c) 11 o'clock   d) 3 o'clock

_____   _____   _____   _____

3. Draw hands on the clock to show the time.

a)

7:00

b)

2 o'clock

c)

3 o'clock

d)

4:00

BONUS ▶

e)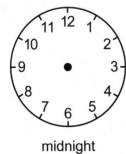

midnight

f)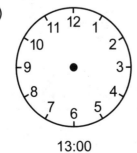

13:00

g)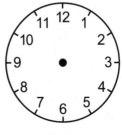

16:00

h)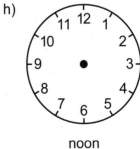

noon

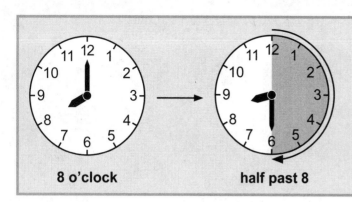

8 o'clock   **half past 8**

It is half an hour after 8:00.
The hour hand is between 8 and 9.
The time is **half past** 8.

$60 \div 2 = 30$, so the time is 8:30.

4. Write the time two ways.

a)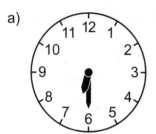

half past ___6___

____ : ____

b)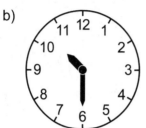

half past _____

____ : ____

c)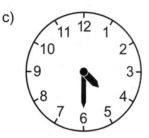

half past _____

____ : ____

d)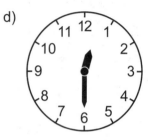

half past _____

____ : ____

5. Write the time in numbers.

a) half past 7

_____

b) half past 5

_____

c) half past 11

_____

d) half past 3

_____

6. Draw hands on the clock to show the time.

a)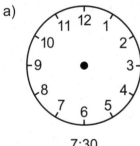

7:30

b)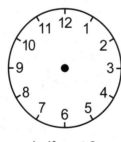

half past 2

c)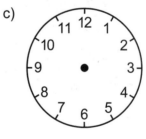

30 minutes after 3

d)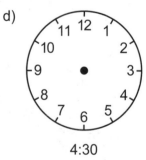

4:30

BONUS ▶

e)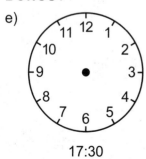

17:30

f)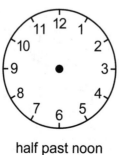

half past noon

g)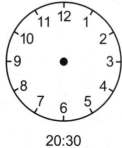

20:30

h)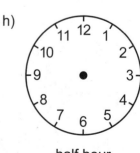

half hour
to midnight

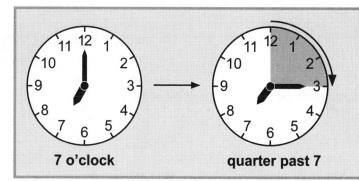

7 o'clock   quarter past 7

It is a quarter of an hour after 7:00 or **quarter past** 7.

$60 \div 4 = 15$, so the time is 7:15.

7. Write the time in words and numbers. Use "quarter" in your answer.

a)

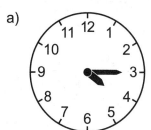

_____

_____

b)

_____

_____

c)

_____

_____

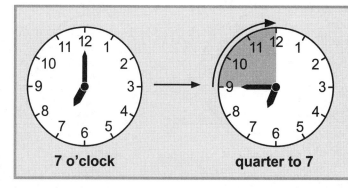

7 o'clock   quarter to 7

It is a quarter of an hour before 7:00 or **quarter to** 7.

The time is 6:45.

8. Write the time in words and numbers. Use "quarter" in your answer.

a)

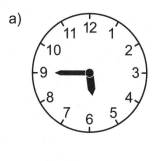

_____

_____

b)

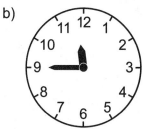

_____

_____

c)

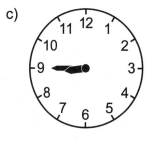

_____

_____

9. Write the time in numbers.

a) quarter past 7

_____

b) quarter to 7

_____

c) quarter past 11

_____

d) quarter to 11

_____

e) quarter past 1

_____

f) quarter to 4

_____

g) quarter to 9

_____

h) quarter past 5

_____

i) half past 9

_____

j) quarter to 12

_____

k) half past 2

_____

l) quarter past 3

_____

10. Draw hands on the clock to show the time.

a)
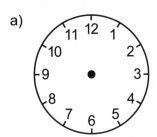

7:15

b)
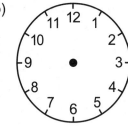

9:15

c)
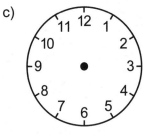

quarter past 4

d)
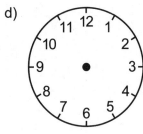

quarter past 6

e)
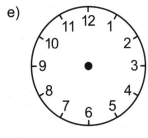

10:45

f)
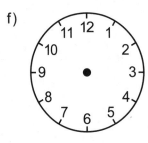

8:45

g)
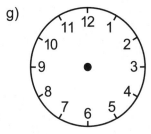

quarter to 4

h)
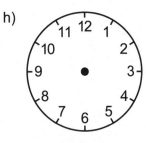

quarter to 6

i)
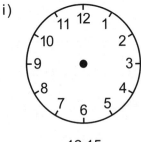

12:15

j)

22:45

k)
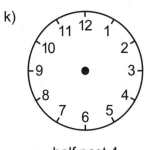

half past 4

l)
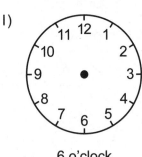

6 o'clock

11. Is the hour hand closer to 4 or to 5 …

a) at 4:15?

_____

b) at 4:45?

_____

BONUS ▶ at 4:30?

_____

ME4-24 Telling Time to Five Minutes

What time is it?

Step 1: Look at the hour hand. It points between 4 and 5. The hour is 4.

Step 2: Look at the minute hand. It points at 2. Skip count by 5s or multiply by 5 to find the minutes: 5, 10, or 2 × 5 = 10.

The time is 4:10.

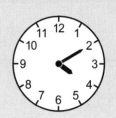

1. What time is it?

a)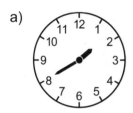

       _1_ : _40_

b)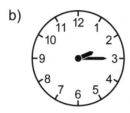

       _____ : _____

c)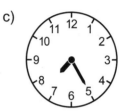

       _____ : _____

d)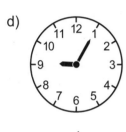

       _____ : _____

e)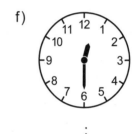

       _____ : _____

f)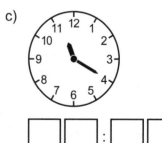

       _____ : _____

2. Write the time on the digital clock.

a)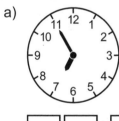

0	6	:	5	5

b)

c)

d)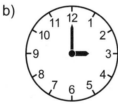

e)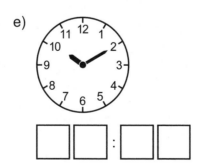

f)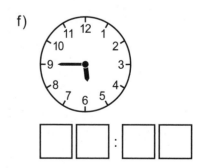

3. Write the time two ways.

a)

6:45

quarter to 7

b)

_____

_____

c)

_____

_____

d)

_____

_____

e)

_____

_____

f)

_____

_____

4. Draw hands on the clock to show the time.

a)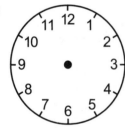

7:10

b)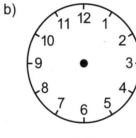

9:40

c)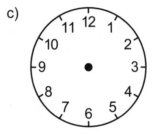

11:05

d)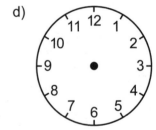

2:45

e)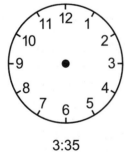

3:35

f)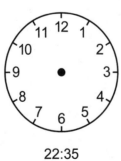

22:35

g)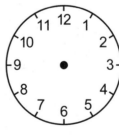

20:20

h)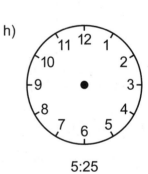

5:25

5. Write the time in Question 4, part f) as many ways as you can.

_____

_____

ME4-25 Telling Time to the Minute

Each division on the clock stands for 1 minute.

The minute hand is pointing between the 4 and the 5.
Count by 5s until you reach the 4: twenty minutes have passed.
Then count on by ones: two minutes have passed.

$20 + 2 = 22$ minutes have passed

It is **7:22** or **22 minutes after 7**.

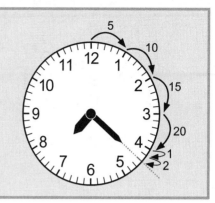

1. How many minutes past the hour is it?

a)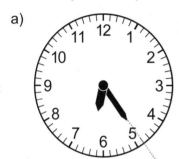

_____24_____ minutes past

b)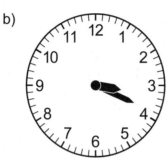

_____ minutes past

c)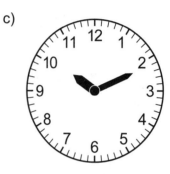

_____ minutes past

d)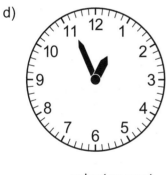

_____ minutes past

e)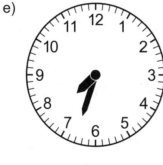

_____ minutes past

f)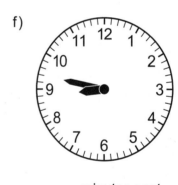

_____ minutes past

2. What time is it?

a)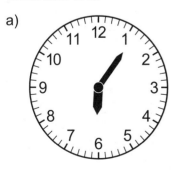

_____ minutes past _____

b)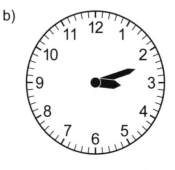

_____ minutes past _____

c)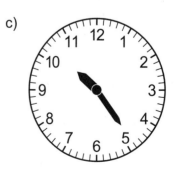

_____ minutes past _____

3. Write the exact time.

a)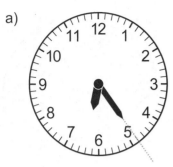

<u> 6 </u> : <u> 24 </u>

b)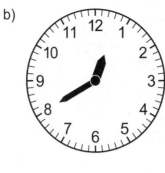

_____ : _____

c)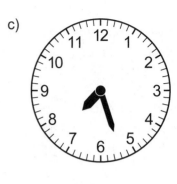

_____ : _____

d)

_____ : _____

e)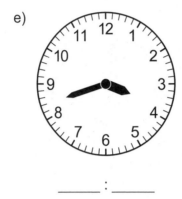

_____ : _____

f)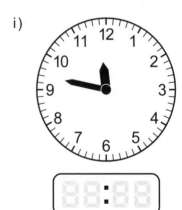

_____ : _____

BONUS ▶

g)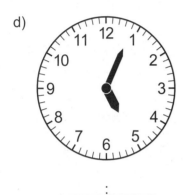

h)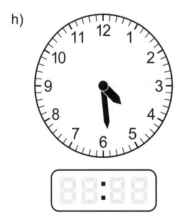

i)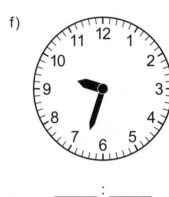

j)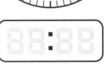

k)

l)

The minute hand is pointing between the 8 and the 9.
To say how many minutes to the hour:

   Count by 5s until you reach the 9. Then count on by ones.

   $15 + 2 = 17$ minutes are left before the next hour.

It is **17 minutes to 7**.

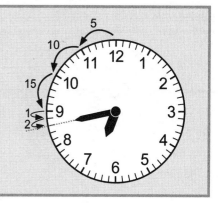

4. How many minutes to the hour is it?

a)

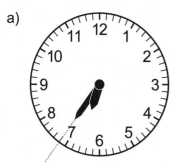

_24_ minutes to 7

b)

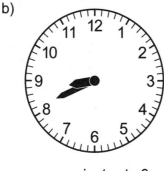

_____ minutes to 9

c)

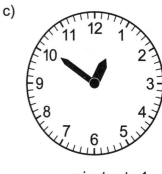

_____ minutes to 1

5. What time is it?

a)

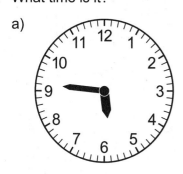

_____ minutes to _____

b)

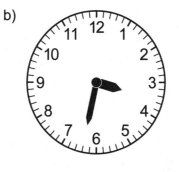

_____ minutes to _____

c)

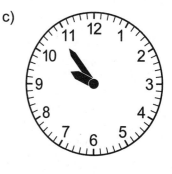

_____ minutes to _____

d)

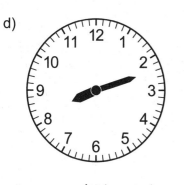

_____ minutes past _____

e)

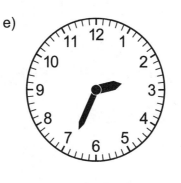

_____ minutes to _____

f)

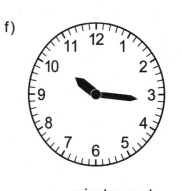

_____ minutes past _____

6. Tell the time two ways.

a)

b)

c)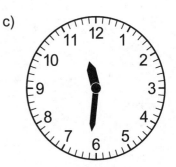

a) _____ minutes past _____

_____ minutes to _____

b) _____ minutes past _____

_____ minutes to _____

c) _____ minutes past _____

_____ minutes to _____

REMINDER ▶ 1 hour = 60 minutes.

It is 4:35. This is 35 minutes past 4.

How much time is left till 5 o'clock?

60 − 35 = 25, so it is 25 minutes to 5.

---

7. Tell the time two ways.

a) `3:40`

b) `10:51`

c) `5:39`

a) _____ minutes past _____

_____ minutes to _____

b) _____ minutes past _____

_____ minutes to _____

c) _____ minutes past _____

_____ minutes to _____

8. Write the time in numbers.

a) twenty minutes after five __*5*__ : __*20*__

b) quarter past eleven _____ : _____

c) three fifty-six _____ : _____

d) eight thirty _____ : _____

e) forty-one minutes after seven _____ : _____

f) quarter to nine _____ : _____

BONUS ▶

g) twenty-three minutes to four _____ : _____

h) nineteen minutes to twelve _____ : _____

BONUS ▶ Write the time shown on the clock three different ways.

_____

_____

_____

Measurement 4-25

ME4-26 Time Intervals

1. Count by 5s to find the time interval.

a) 8:10 to 8:25

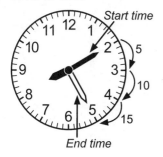

Start time

5

10

15

End time

15 minutes

b) 3:15 to 3:40

_____

c) 10:25 to 11:00

_____

d) 7:35 to 8:00

_____

e) 3:40 to 4:05

_____

f) 9:25 to 10:20

_____

2. Count by 5s and then by 1s to find how much time has elapsed.

a) 8:35 to 8:57

_____

b) 4:30 to 5:04

_____

c) 6:20 to 7:17

_____

d) 4:20 to 4:57

_____

e) 1:15 to 1:31

_____

f) 5:40 to 6:19

_____

3. Count by 5s to find the time interval.

a) 1:12 to 1:52

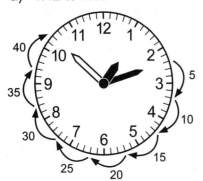

_____

b) 6:18 to 6:43

_____

c) 7:49 to 8:09

_____

4. Count by 5s and then by 1s to find the time interval.

a) 3:14 to 3:47

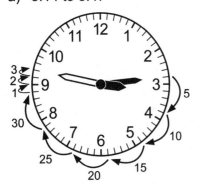

_____

b) 11:36 to 11:54

_____

c) 4:48 to 5:12

_____

5. Count by 5s to estimate the time interval. Then find the actual time interval.

a) 2:47 to 3:15

Estimate:

_____

Actual:

_____

b) 4:33 to 4:59

Estimate:

_____

Actual:

_____

c) 9:21 to 9:38

Estimate:

_____

Actual:

_____

6. It is now 5:13. Matt started playing at 4:21. How long has he been playing?

7. The clock shows the time Kate started reading. At what time did she finish reading?
Draw an arrow on the clock to show the time she finished.

a) Kate read for 20 minutes.   b) Kate read for 15 minutes.   c) Kate read for 23 minutes.

Kate finished at _____.   Kate finished at _____.   Kate finished at _____.

Jake started reading at 1:21. He read for 36 minutes. When did he finish reading?

```
  1:21  ◄────── start time
+ 0:36  ◄────── elapsed time = 36 minutes = 0 hours 36 minutes = 0:36
──────
  1:57
```

Jake finished reading at 1:57.

---

8. Add to find the end time.

a)	b)	c)	d)	e)
3:23	8:22	1:48	6:37	3:42
+ 0:20	+ 0:11	+ 5:00	+ 2:15	+ 8:09

9. Regroup 60 minutes as 1 hour.

a) 2:65
   3:05
b) 7:71
c) 8:80
d) 2:92
e) 1:105

10. Add and regroup to find the end time.

a)	b)	c)	d)	e)
3:23	8:22	9:48	6:43	3:42
+ 1:40	+ 0:51	+ 1:30	+ 2:25	+ 1:50
4:63				
5:03				

11. a) Nina goes to bed at 7:45 p.m. Evan's bedtime is 30 minutes later.
What time does Evan go to bed?

b) Tess put chicken in the oven at 4:52 p.m. It should bake for 1 hour and 40 minutes.
At what time should she take it out?

12. Cody started reading at 3:33. He finished at 4:27. How long was he reading?

BONUS ▶ Muffins need to bake for 22 minutes. You want them to be ready at 6:00 p.m.
When should you put the muffins into the oven?

ME4-27 Elapsed Time

1. Find how much time has passed between the times in bold (intervals are not shown to scale).

a)

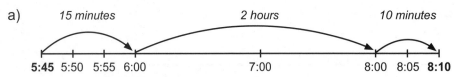

Elapsed time: *2 hours 25 minutes*

b)

Elapsed time: _____

c)

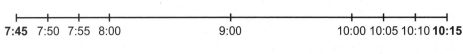

Elapsed time: _____

2. Find how much time has passed between the times in bold.
   Regroup 60 minutes as 1 hour.

a)

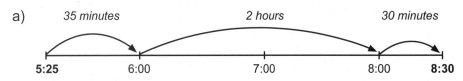

Elapsed time: *2 hours 65 minutes = 3 hours 5 minutes*

b)

Elapsed time: _____

c)

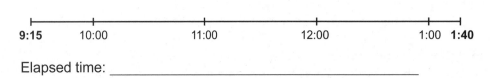

Elapsed time: _____

3. Draw a timeline to find out how much time has elapsed between …

   a) 7:40 and 10:10   b) 4:35 and 6:05   c) 8:50 and 10:10

122

Measurement 4-27

4. Draw a timeline to find the arrival time.

a) Sun leaves home at 8:15 a.m. and walks 20 minutes to get to school.

She arrives at _____ .

|———————————————————————————————|

b) Ben leaves home at 8:25 a.m. He walks 10 minutes to the bus. The bus drives 25 minutes to get to school.

Ben arrives at school at _____ .

|———————————————————————————————|

c) Emma wakes up at 6:30 a.m. She takes 15 minutes to eat breakfast, exercises for 1 hour, takes 35 minutes to shower, dress, and brush her teeth, and then takes another 25 minutes to get to school.

Emma gets to school at _____ .

|———————————————————————————————|

5. The movie starts at 7:00 p.m. Will the student be on time? Estimate your answer, then use a timeline or add the times to check.

a) Marla eats dinner at 6:00 p.m. It takes 25 minutes. Then she brushes her teeth for 5 minutes. She walks 5 minutes to the bus stop. She waits 5 minutes for the bus. The bus ride to the movie theatre takes 15 minutes.

b) David leaves his home at 5:45 p.m. and walks 10 minutes to Ken's. Ken takes 5 minutes to get ready. Then they walk together 20 minutes to Hanna's. Hanna is waiting outside when Ken and David arrive. All three walk 10 minutes to a pizzeria. They wait 10 minutes in line and then 5 minutes to get their pizza. They take 15 minutes to eat their pizza. They then walk another 10 minutes to the movie theatre.

c) Mary starts her homework at 11:00 a.m. She studies for 2 hours, then takes a 90 minute break to have lunch and relax. Then she has dance class. Mary is home from dance class after 2 hours. Mary does 1 more hour of schoolwork before stopping for dinner. Helping with dinner, eating, and cleaning up takes 1 hour and 15 minutes. Her father takes 10 minutes to drive her to the movie theatre.

ME4-28 Dates

1. Write the months in order.

June, **February**, **April**, **January**, **December**, **May**, **March**, **November**, **August**, **October**, **July**, **September**

01: _____ 02: _____ 03: _____ 04: _____

05: _____ 06: _____ 07: _____ 08: _____

09: _____ 10: _____ 11: _____ 12: _____

2. Give the number of each month. Write "0" in front of any one-digit numbers.

May: __05__   August: _____   June: _____   January: _____   October: _____

December: _____   February: _____   November: _____   April: _____   July: _____

3. Write the date as day month year. Then rewrite the date using two-digit days and months.

a) June 8, 1963

_____ 8 June 1963 _____

__08__ / __06__ / __1963__
  dd / mm / yyyy

b) April 9, 1976

_____

_____ / _____ / _____
 dd / mm / yyyy

c) May 24, 2001

_____

_____ / _____ / _____
 dd / mm / yyyy

d) December 25, 2015

_____

_____ / _____ / _____

e) September 29, 2010

_____

_____ / _____ / _____

f) July 1, 1867

_____

_____ / _____ / _____

4. Write the date as day month year using two-digit days, months, and years.

a) June 8, 1963

__08__ / __06__ / __63__
  dd / mm / yy

b) March 5, 1976

_____ / _____ / _____
 dd / mm / yy

c) May 24, 2001

_____ / _____ / _____
 dd / mm / yy

d) October 11, 1358

_____ / _____ / _____

e) August 4, 1971

_____ / _____ / _____

f) November 9, 1999

_____ / _____ / _____

BONUS ▶

a) What is the shortest month of the year? _____

b) How many days are in the longest month? _____

5. Write the date as year month day using only numbers.

a) June 8, 1963

_____ - _____ - _____
  yyyy - mm - dd

b) August 29, 1968

_____ - _____ - _____
  yyyy - mm - dd

c) January 1, 2009

_____ - _____ - _____
  yyyy - mm - dd

d) February 23, 1411

_____ - _____ - _____

e) November 1, 2010

_____ - _____ - _____

f) April 8, 1065

_____ - _____ - _____

6. Write the date in words.

a) 1982-07-25 _____

b) 1999-12-31 _____

c) 2001-06-01 _____

d) 2020-05-07 _____

e) 1977-10-17 _____

f) 1981-03-08 _____

7. On what day of the week is the date?

May 2018

Sunday	Monday	Tuesday	Wednesday	Thursday	Friday	Saturday
		1	2	3	4	5
6	7	8	9	10	11	12
13	14	15	16	17	18	19
20	21	22	23	24	25	26
27	28	29	30	31		

a) May 5, 2018 _____

b) 2018-05-22 _____

c) 17/05/18 _____

d) 05/16/18 _____

e) 09/05/2018 _____

BONUS ▶ 02/06/2018 _____

8. List all the dates you can write as 05/08/11.

_____   _____   _____

_____   _____   _____

9. Why do we need a standard way to write dates? Give an example.

ME4-29 Longer Periods of Time

1. Fill in the table.

Days	1	2	3	4	5
Hours	24				

2. Write the time in days and hours.

a) 27 hours = ___1___ day and _____ hours   b) 50 hours = _____ days and _____ hours

c) 100 hours = _____ days and _____ hours   d) 75 hours = _____ days and _____ hours

3. a) Fill in the table.

Weeks	1	2	3	4	5	6	7
Days							

b) What number do you multiply by to get the number of days from the number of weeks? _____

4. Change the time expressed in weeks and days to days only.

a) 2 weeks, 3 days   b) 2 weeks, 5 days   c) 3 weeks, 2 days

= _____ days + _____ days   = _____ days + _____ days   = _____ days + _____ days

= _____ days   = _____ days   = _____ days

5. A month can have 28, 29, 30, or 31 days. About how many full weeks are in 1 month?

6. Fill in the table.

Years	1	2	3	4	5
Months	12				

7. Change the time expressed in years and months to months only.

a) 2 years, 3 months   b) 1 year, 5 months   c) 3 years, 11 months

= ____ months + ____ months   = ____ months + ____ months   = ____ months + ____ months

= ____ months   = ____ months   = ____ months

A **decade** is 10 years. A **century** is 100 years.

8. Fill in the blanks.

   a) 60 years = _____ decades

   b) 800 years = _____ centuries

   c) 12 decades = _____ years

   d) 40 decades = _____ centuries

9. Circle the longer interval. Explain your answer.

   a) 7 decades   OR   85 years

   b) 8 centuries   OR   670 years

10. Canada became a country in 1867.

   a) About how many centuries ago was this?

   b) About how many decades ago was this?

11. A family has 2 weeks plus 2 extra days to spend on vacation. They want to divide their time equally between family and friends in 4 different cities. How much time can they spend in each city?

12. Most students spend about 9 months of the year in school.

   a) How many months will most students spend in school from Grades 1 to 6?

   b) How many years will most students spend in school from Grades 1 to 6?

13. A university term is 4 months long. Most university students are in school for a total of 8 terms. How many years do students study in total?

14. The Tran family leaves for summer vacation on July 5. They drive for 2 days to a friend's house, where they stay for 1 week. They drive 1 day to another friend's house, where they stay for 4 days. They then take 2 days to drive home. On what day does the Tran family arrive home?

   BONUS ▶ How many days of summer vacation are left before school starts on September 2? How many weeks?

G4-10 3-D Shapes

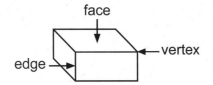 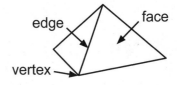
1. What is the shape of the shaded face?

a)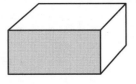

b)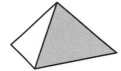

c)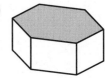

_____

_____

_____

d)

e)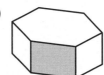

BONUS ▶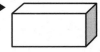

_____

_____

_____

2. Draw a dot on each vertex you see.

a)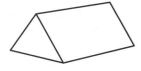

b)

c)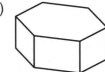

3. Trace the edges you see.

a)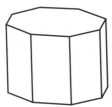

b)

c)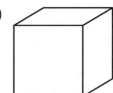

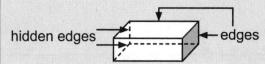

Faces meet at **edges**. Hidden edges are shown with dashed lines.

hidden edges → ← edges

4. Draw dashed lines to show the hidden edges.

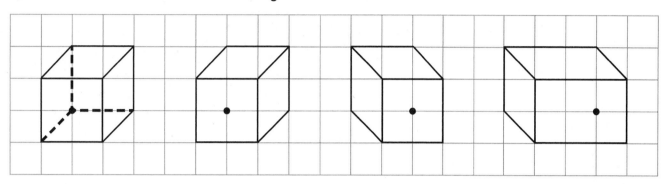

5. Trace and count the edges.

a)

_____ edges

b)

_____ edges

c)

_____ edges

d)

_____ edges

6. Draw a dot on each vertex. Count the vertices.

a)

_____ vertices

b)

_____ vertices

c)

_____ vertices

d)

_____ vertices

7. Imagine the shape is placed on a table. Trace the edges that would be hidden.

a)

b)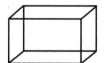

c)

d)

G4-11 Triangular and Rectangular Prisms

Prisms have two identical opposite faces called **bases**.

The bases of **triangular** prisms are triangles.

 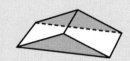

The bases of **rectangular** prisms are rectangles.

On rectangular prisms, any pair of opposite faces can be called bases.

1. Shade the bases of the prism. Then name the prism.

a)

b)

c)

d)

_____triangular_____

_____prism_____

    _____

    _____

    _____

    _____

    _____

    _____

2. Cross out the objects that are not prisms. Shade the bases of the triangular prisms.
Circle the rectangular prisms.

 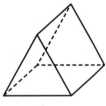   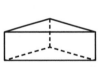 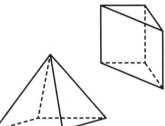

To make a skeleton of a prism:

Step 1
Make two copies of the same polygon using clay balls for vertices and toothpicks for edges. They are the bases of the prism.

Step 2
Add a toothpick to each vertex of one of the bases.

Step 3
Attach the other base on top of the toothpicks.

3. Fill in the table using skeletons of prisms.

Shape of Base	triangle	rectangle	square
Number of Vertices			
Number of Edges			

COPYRIGHT © 2018 JUMP MATH: NOT TO BE COPIED.

4. Connect the matching vertices with edges to finish drawing the skeleton of the prism.

a) 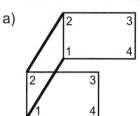 b) 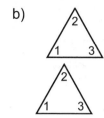 c)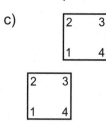

5. Draw the skeleton of a rectangular prism by following these steps:

Step 1: Draw the two identical rectangular bases, a little bit apart and to the side.

Step 2: Connect the vertices of the bases in pairs: the bottom-left corner of one base goes to the bottom-left corner of the other, and so on.

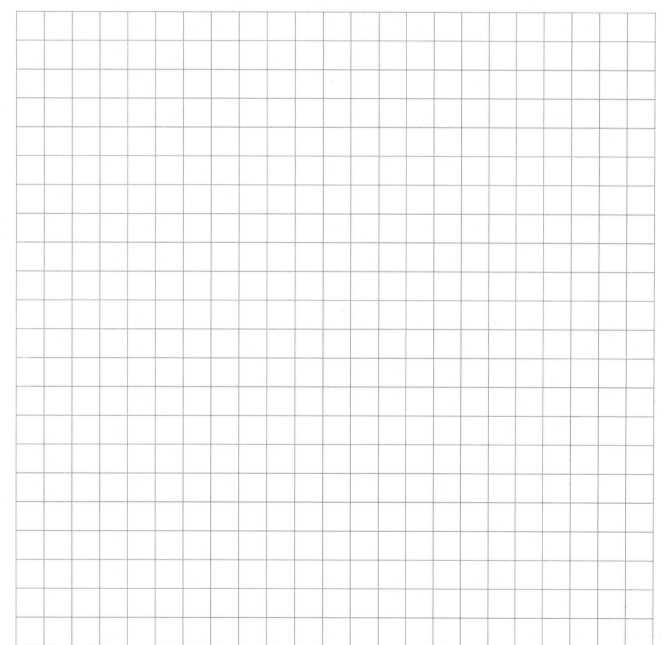

G4-12 Nets of Prisms

1. a) Complete the table.

Shape	Name of Shape	Number of ...			Picture of Faces
		Vertices	**Edges**	**Faces**	

b) Count the number of sides in the base of each prism. Compare this number to the number of vertices in each prism. What do you notice?

_____

_____

c) The faces that are not bases are called **side faces**.

The side faces of these prisms are _____ .

2. Match the net to the 3-D object.

A. **B.** **C.** **D.** **E.**

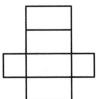 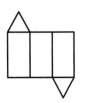 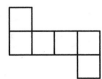 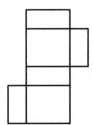

a)   b)   c)   d)   e)

___   ___   ___   ___   ___

G4-13 Prisms

REMINDER ▶ Any polygon can be the base of a prism. Examples:

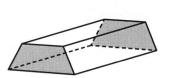
trapezoid-based prism

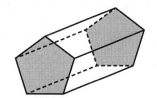
pentagon-based prism

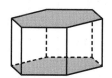
hexagon-based prism

1. Shade a base of the prism. Then name the prism.

a)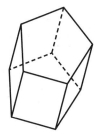

_____-based prism

b)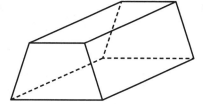

_____-based prism

c)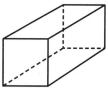

_____-based prism

d)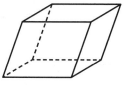

_____-based prism

e)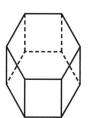

_____-based prism

f)

_____-based prism

To make a skeleton of a prism:

Step 1
Make two copies of the same polygon using clay balls for vertices and toothpicks for edges. They are the bases of the prism.

Step 2
Add a toothpick to each vertex of one of the bases.

Step 3
Attach the other base on top of the toothpicks.

---

2. Build the skeletons of three prisms with the following bases: trapezoids, pentagons, and hexagons.

3. Use the skeletons you made in Question 2 to fill in the table.

Shape of Base	Number of ...			Picture of Faces
	Vertices	Edges	Faces	
trapezoid				
pentagon				
hexagon				

4. Use pattern blocks to build a prism with a parallelogram as its base.

a) How many vertices does your prism have? _____

b) How many edges does your prism have? _____

c) How many faces does your prism have? _____

d) Draw the faces.

BONUS ▶ A prism has an 8-sided base.

How many rectangular faces does the prism have? _____

How many vertices does the prism have? _____

How many edges does the prism have? _____

G4-14 Pyramids

Pyramids have one base and a vertex opposite to the base.

The bases of **triangular** pyramids are triangles.   The bases of **rectangular** pyramids are rectangles.

Any face of a triangular pyramid can be called a base.

1. Shade the base and draw a dot on the vertex opposite the base. Then name the pyramid.

a)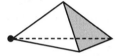

b)

c)

d)

____triangular____

____pyramid____

_____

_____

_____

_____

_____

_____

2. Shade the base or bases. Then name the base and write "prism" or "pyramid."

a)

b)

c)

d)

_____

_____

_____

_____

_____

_____

_____

_____

e)

f)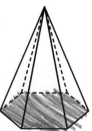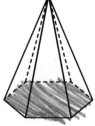

g)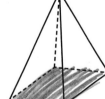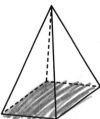

h)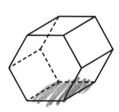

_____

_____

_____

_____

_____

_____

_____

_____

COPYRIGHT © 2018 JUMP MATH: NOT TO BE COPIED.

A skeleton of a 3-D shape has only edges and vertices.

To make a skeleton of a pyramid:

Step 1: Make a polygon using clay balls for vertices and toothpicks for edges. The polygon is the base of the pyramid.

Step 2: Add a toothpick to each vertex.

Step 3: Join the loose toothpicks to make one vertex at the top.

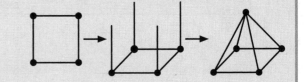

3. a) Build the skeletons of three pyramids with the following bases: triangle, square, pentagon.

   b) Sketch the skeletons of your pyramids by following these steps.

   Step 1: Draw the base.

   Step 2: Draw the extra vertex.

   Step 3: Connect the vertices of the base to the extra vertex.

4. a) Complete the table. Use actual 3-D shapes to help you.

Shape	Name of Shape	Number of ...			Picture of Faces
		Vertices	Edges	Faces	
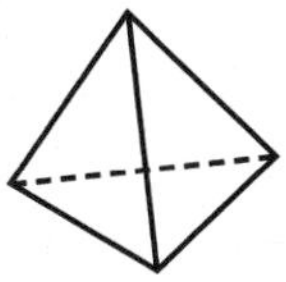					
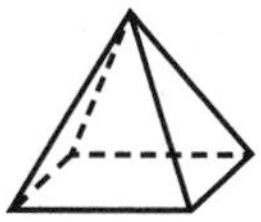					

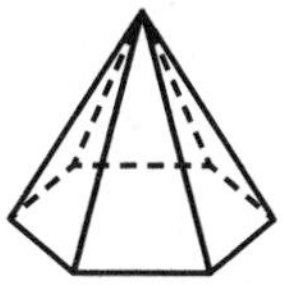					

b) Circle the bases in the last column of the table.

c) The side faces of these pyramids are _____.

5. An object has a 7-sided base and 8 vertices. Is it a prism or a pyramid? Explain.

_____

_____

_____

6. What 3-D shape can you make using only congruent triangles as faces?

BONUS ▶

a) An object has 9 vertices and 16 edges. Is it a pyramid or a prism? How many sides does its base have?

b) An object has 14 vertices and 21 edges. Is it a pyramid or a prism? How many sides does its base have?

1. Match the net to the 3-D object.

A. 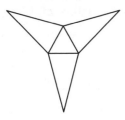   B. 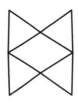   C.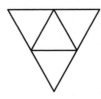

a)   b)   c)

_____   _____   _____

2. Does the net make a cube? Write "yes" or "no."

a) 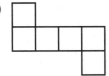   b) 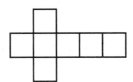   c)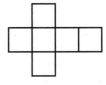

_____   _____   _____

d) 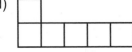   e) 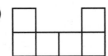   f)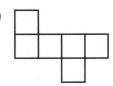

_____   _____   _____

3. Does the net make a square-based pyramid? Write "yes" or "no."

a)   b)   c)   d)

_____   _____   _____   _____

4. Draw the missing face for the net.

a)   b)   c) 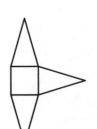   d)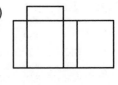

5. Create a net for the object.

a)

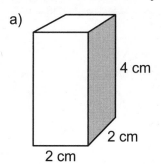

b)

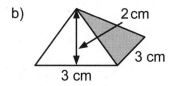

G4-16 Volume

Volume is the amount of space taken up by a three-dimensional (or 3-D) object.
These objects have a volume of 4 cubes.

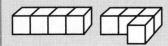

1. Count the number of cubes to find the volume.

a)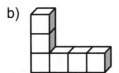

Volume = _____ cubes

b)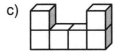

Volume = _____ cubes

c)

Volume = _____ cubes

d)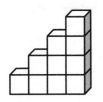

Volume = _____ cubes

e)

Volume = _____ cubes

f)

Volume = _____ cubes

g)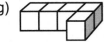

Volume = _____ cubes

h)

Volume = _____ cubes

i)

Volume = _____ cubes

2. How many cubes are in the shaded row?

a)

_____ cubes

b)

_____ cubes

c)

_____ cubes

3. How many cubes are in the shaded layer?

a)

_____ cubes

b)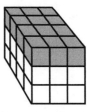

_____ cubes

c)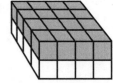

_____ cubes

4. How many layers are there like the shaded layer?

a)

_____ layers

b)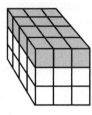

_____ layers

c)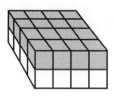

_____ layers

5. Multiply the number of blocks in the shaded layer by the number of layers to find the volume.

a)

Volume = _____ × _____

= _____ cubes

b)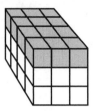

Volume = _____ × _____

= _____ cubes

c)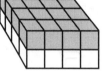

Volume = _____ × _____

= _____ cubes

d)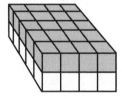

Volume = _____ × _____

= _____ cubes

e)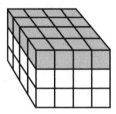

Volume = _____ × _____

= _____ cubes

f)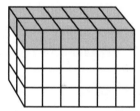

Volume = _____ × _____

= _____ cubes

6. Find the volume.

a)

Volume = _____ cubes

b)

Volume = _____ cubes

c)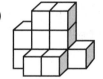

Volume = _____ cubes

G4-17 Capacity

> The **capacity** of a container is how much it can hold.

1. Circle the container with greater capacity in real life.

a)

b)

c)

> Capacity is measured in **litres** (**L**).
>
> 4 cups together make about 1 L.
>
>

2. Circle the objects that have capacity less than 1 L. Cross out the objects that have capacity more than 1 L.

3. The milk carton has a capacity of 1 L. Estimate the capacity of the other container.

a)

Capacity = _____ L

b)

Capacity = _____ L

c)

Capacity = _____ L

> The volume of a liquid is also measured in litres.
>
> The container has a capacity of 4 L. The water in the container has a volume of 3 L.
>
>

4. Find the capacity of the container and the volume of the liquid.

a)

Capacity = _____ L

Volume = _____ L

b)

Capacity = _____ L

Volume = _____ L

c)

Capacity = _____ L

Volume = _____ L

COPYRIGHT © 2018 JUMP MATH: NOT TO BE COPIED.

5. a) Ronin says he drank 1 L of juice without stopping. Is that reasonable?

Explain. _____

b) Marla says she needs 1 L of water to take a bath. Is that reasonable?

Explain. _____

Small quantities of liquid are measured in **millilitres** (**mL**). One teaspoon holds 5 mL of liquid.

---

6. Circle the best unit to measure the capacity of the object.

a) a large can of paint

mL   L

b) a raindrop

mL   L

c) a bathtub

mL   L

d) a medicine bottle

mL   L

e) a bucket of ice cream

mL   L

f) a cup of tea

mL   L

7. Clara filled a measuring cup with 40 mL of water. She poured out some water. There was 30 mL left. How much water did she pour out?

_____

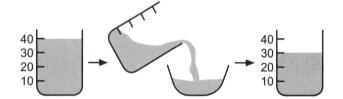

8. The juice box holds 200 mL. Estimate the capacity of the other container.

a)

_____ mL

b)

_____ mL

c)

_____ mL

BONUS ▶ A 1 cm connecting cube filled with water holds 1 mL. How much water would the 3-D shape hold?

a)

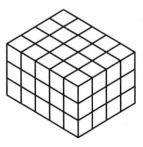

Capacity = _____ mL

b)

Capacity = _____ mL

G4-18 Litres and Millilitres

> **REMINDER** ▶ There are 1000 millilitres in 1 litre. 1 L = 1000 mL.

1. Fill in the table.

L	1	2	3	4	5	6	7	8
mL	*1000*							

2. Sort the containers in order of increasing capacity.

A.   B.   C.   D.   E.   F.

_____   _____   _____   _____   _____   _____

smallest   largest

3. How many containers hold 1 L?

a) 100 mL yogourt cup × _____10_____ = 1 L   b) 200 mL juice box × _____ = 1 L

c) 250 mL cup × _____ = 1 L   d) 500 mL soup can × _____ = 1 L

BONUS ▶ Write a multiplication sentence to explain your answer to part c).

_____

4. Amir has a fish tank that holds 20 L of water. To keep fish healthy, it is recommended that 30 g of salt be added for every 40 L of water. How much salt should Amir add to his tank?

BONUS ▶ If Amir changes the water in his tank every 3 months, how long will a 300 g container of salt last?

BONUS ▶ Change the following measurements to millilitres.

a) 3 L = _____ mL   b) 9 L = _____ mL   c) 12 L = _____ mL   d) 50 L = _____ mL

PDM4-10 Outcomes

When you flip a coin, the result is one of two possible **outcomes.**
There is never more than one **result** for each flip.

When Alice plays a game of cards with a friend, the result will be one of three possible outcomes:

    1. Alice wins.

    2. Alice loses.

    3. Nobody wins or loses.

1. List all the outcomes (possible results) of spinning the spinner in the table. How many outcomes are there in total?

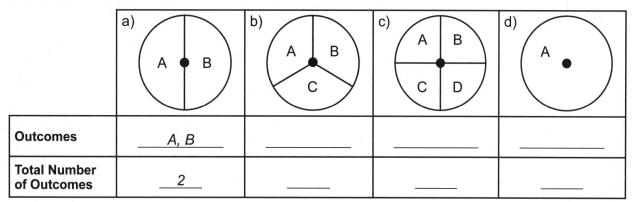

	a)	b)	c)	d)
Outcomes	_A, B_	_____	_____	_____
Total Number of Outcomes	_2_	_____	_____	_____

2. If you spin any spinner from Question 1 exactly once, how many results will there be? _____

3. Fill in the chart.

		Outcomes	Total Number of Outcomes
a)	**Tossing a Coin**		
b)	**Rolling a Six-Sided Die**		

4. You take one ball out of the box. List the outcomes. How many outcomes are there?

a)

    outcomes: _Y, R_

    _2_ outcomes

b)

    outcomes: _____

    _____ outcomes

c)

    outcomes: _____

    _____ outcome

d)

    outcomes: _____

    _____ outcomes

Spinning the spinner on the right has four outcomes:

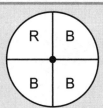

1. The pointer lands in the top right. (B)
2. The pointer lands in the bottom right. (B)
3. The pointer lands in the bottom left. (B)
4. The pointer lands in the top left. (R)

5. How many outcomes are there in total? How many red outcomes are there?

a) 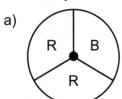   _____ outcomes

_____ red outcomes

b) 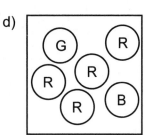   _____ outcomes

_____ red outcomes

c) 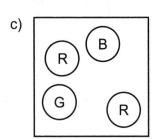   _____ outcomes

_____ red outcomes

d)   _____ outcomes

_____ red outcomes

6. Fill in the chart.

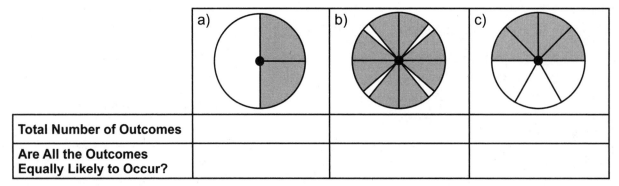

	a)	b)	c)
Total Number of Outcomes			
Are All the Outcomes Equally Likely to Occur?			

7. Draw different-coloured buttons in the box. There should be eight outcomes in total, and three outcomes should be for a yellow button.

Probability and Data Management 4-10

Expectations for Simple Events

> The spinner has two outcomes. There is an equal chance of spinning grey or white.
>
> We expect to spin grey
> $\frac{1}{2}$ of the time.
>
>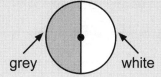
> grey   white
>
> We expect to spin white
> $\frac{1}{2}$ of the time.

1. a) Fill in the chart.

	i)	ii)	iii)	BONUS ▶
Total Number of Outcomes	2			
Number of Grey Outcomes	1			
Number of White Outcomes	1			
Fraction of Grey Outcomes	$\frac{1}{2}$			
Fraction of White Outcomes	$\frac{1}{2}$			

   b) Lewis spins each spinner in part a) 20 times. How many times does he expect it to land on each colour?

   i) grey __10__ white __10__   ii) grey _____ white _____

   iii) grey _____ white _____   **BONUS ▶** grey _____ white _____

2. a) If you flip a coin repeatedly, what fraction of the time would you expect it to land on each side?

   heads [ ]   tails [ ]

   b) Is there an equal chance of getting heads or tails? _____

3. Thirty students each flipped the same coin 100 times, so altogether it was flipped 3000 times. On every flip, it landed with heads facing up. How can you explain what happened?

   _____

   _____

There are four outcomes for this spinner: one is for grey and three are for white.

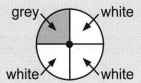

We expect to spin grey
$\frac{1}{4}$ of the time.

We expect to spin white
$\frac{3}{4}$ of the time.

4. a) How many times do you expect grey when you spin the spinner …

    i) 4 times? ___1___   ii) 8 times? _____   iii) 12 times? _____

    iv) 16 times? _____   v) 20 times? _____   vi) 24 times? _____

  b) How many times do you expect white when you spin the spinner …

    i) 4 times? ___3___   ii) 8 times? _____   iii) 12 times? _____

    iv) 16 times? _____   v) 20 times? _____   vi) 24 times? _____

  c) i) Is there an equal chance for the spinner to land on white or grey? _____

    ii) Are the chances of landing on white or grey the same? _____

There are six outcomes when you roll a die: two are for numbers less than 3 (1, 2), and four are for numbers greater than 2 (3, 4, 5, 6).

We expect to roll a
number less than 3
$\frac{2}{6}$ of the time.

We expect to roll a
number greater than 2
$\frac{4}{6}$ of the time.

5. a) How many times do you expect to get a number less than 3 when you roll a die …

    i) 6 times? _____   ii) 12 times? _____   iii) 18 times? _____

  b) How many times do you expect to get a number greater than 2 when you roll a die …

    i) 6 times? _____   ii) 12 times? _____   iii) 18 times? _____

BONUS ▶ Shade any two of the numbers so that $\frac{2}{6}$ of the numbers are shaded and $\frac{4}{6}$ are not shaded.

  a) How many times do you expect to get a shaded number when you roll a die ...

    i) 6 times? _____   ii) 12 times? _____   iii) 18 times? _____

  b) How many times do you expect to get an unshaded number when you roll a die ...

    i) 6 times? _____   ii) 12 times? _____   iii) 18 times? _____

PDM4-12 Expectations for Compound Events

1. a) Find all the expected outcomes of flipping two dimes. Draw the missing arrow and fill in the blanks.

Outcome of First Dime	Outcomes of Second Dime	Outcomes of Two Flips
H	H T	_H H_ _____
T	H T	_____ _____

   b) How many ways are there of getting the result?

   i) two heads _____   ii) two tails _____   iii) one head and one tail _____

2. Rani and Tom play a game in which they take turns spinning a spinner twice and add the results. The spinner is divided into two equal parts labelled "1" and "2."

   a) Draw the missing arrows and write the addition statements in the table.

Outcome of First Spin	Outcomes of Second Spin	Outcomes of Sums
1	1 2	_1_ + _1_ = _2_ ____ + ____ = ____
2	1 2	____ + ____ = ____ ____ + ____ = ____

   b) How many ways are there of getting the result?

   i) 2 _____   ii) 3 _____   iii) 4 _____

   c) What fraction of the time will they get the result?

   i) 2 ☐   ii) 3 ☐   iii) 4 ☐

   d) If Rani and Tom take 40 turns total, how many of each result of 2, 3, and 4 can they expect?

   _____

   _____

   _____

3. a) Find all the possible outcomes of flipping three dimes. Draw the missing arrows
and fill in the blanks in the table.

Outcome of First Dime	Outcomes of Second Dime	Outcomes of Third Dime	Outcomes of Three Flips
		H	*HHH*
H	H	T	_____
	T	H	_____
		_____	_____
		_____	_____
	_____	_____	_____
_____	_____	_____	_____
		_____	_____

b) How many ways are there of getting the result?

i) 3 H _____   ii) 2 H and 1 T _____   iii) 2 T and 1 H _____   iv) 3 T _____

c) Which results are equally likely to occur? Use your answers to part b) to answer the question.

_____

d) Which outcomes of three flips are most likely? _____

e) What fraction of the time will you get the result?

i) 3 H ☐   ii) 2 H and 1 T ☐   iii) 2 T and 1 H ☐   iv) 3 T ☐

f) How many of each result do you expect if you do the number of sets of three flips?

i)   8 times   ii) 16 times   iii) 24 times

iv) 32 times   v)   40 times   vi) 80 times

4. Two spinners are divided into three equal parts, labelled 1, 2, and 3.

a) Make a chart to show all the expected outcomes of spinning twice and adding
the results. It should have 3 column headings: Outcome of First Spin,
Outcomes of Second Spin, and Outcomes of Sums.

b) How many ways are there of getting each outcome?

c) What fraction of the time can you expect to get each outcome?

Probability and Data Management 4-12

PDM4-13 Experiments in Probability

1. a) If you flip a coin repeatedly, what fraction of the time would you expect to get the result?

   i) heads ☐   ii) tails ☐

   b) If you flip a coin 30 times, how many times would you expect to get the result?

   i) heads _____   ii) tails _____

   c) Flip a coin 30 times and record the results in the tally chart.

Outcome	Prediction	Tally	Count
heads			
tails			

   d) Did the results match your expectations? Explain.

   _____

   _____

2. Which of the three results from 100 coin flips is most likely? Explain.

   A. 100 heads, 0 tails   **B.** 6 heads, 94 tails   **C.** 61 heads, 39 tails

3. a) If you spin the spinner 20 times, how many times would you expect to spin the colour?

   i) grey _____   ii) white _____

   b) Use a paper clip and pencil as a spinner. Spin 20 times. Record the results.

Outcome	Tally	Count
grey		
white		

   c) Did your results match your expectations? Explain.

   _____

   _____

4. Jin and Cathy play a game with the spinner on the right. For each turn, the player spins twice and adds the numbers.

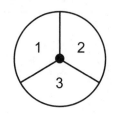

a) Complete the table below to determine how many ways there are of getting the sum.

i) 2 _____   ii) 3 _____   iii) 4 _____

iv) 5 _____   v) 6 _____

Outcome of First Spin	Outcomes of Second Spin	Outcomes of Sums
1	1	_1_ + _1_ = _2_
	2	_____ + _____ = _____
	3	_____ + _____ = _____
2	1	_____ + _____ = _____
	_____	_____ + _____ = _____
	_____	_____ + _____ = _____
3	1	_____ + _____ = _____
	_____	_____ + _____ = _____
	_____	_____ + _____ = _____

b) Which outcomes have an equal chance of occurring? _____

c) Take 18 turns spinning Jin and Cathy's spinner. For each turn, spin the spinner twice and add the outcomes.

d) Record the results from part c) in the table.

Sum	Tally	Count
2		
3		
4		
5		
6		

e) Did your results match your expectations? Explain.

5. Hanna wins if the coin lands on heads. Simon wins if it lands on tails. They flip the coin 20 times altogether and record the results in a tally chart. Hanna says the game was not fair. Do you agree? Explain.

H	ЖÍ III
T	ЖÍ ЖÍ II

Probability and Data Management 4-13